Make Money Self-Publishing

Learn How From Fourteen Successful Small Publishers

by Suzanne P. Thomas

Gemstone House Publishing
PO Box 19948
Boulder, CO 80308
www.GemstoneHouse.com

The following trademarks appear in this book:Bottom/Line Personal Magazine, QuickBooks, Pagemaker, Framemaker, Quark, and Microsoft Word.

Make Money Self-Publishing: Learn How from Fourteen Successful Small Publishers
Copyright © 2001
First Printing 2001

Publisher's Cataloging-in-Publication
(Provided by Quality Books, Inc.)

Thomas, Suzanne P. (Suzanne Patricia), 1965-
    Make money self-publishing: learn how from fourteen successful small publishers / by Suzanne P. Thomas. -- 1 st ed.
    p. cm.
    Includes index.
    Preassigned LCCN:00 091097
    ISBN: 0-9664691-2-7

    1. Self-publishing   I.Title

Z285.5.T56 2000   070.5'93
                    QBI00-500078

Readers are encouraged to contact the publisher with their comments and suggestions for future editions of this book. Please see the feedback contest form at the end of the book.

The author is available for talks on self-publishing. Contact Gemstone House Publishing, 1-800-324-6415.

Acknowledgements:

As always, many people contributed to this book. My thanks especially to the publishers who agreed to be profiled. Their willingness to openly share their experiences will hopefully help many others to succeed in this fascinating business.

Thanks to Shelley Thomas, Jerry Thomas, Cate de la Garza Millard, and Jane Heim for reviewing the manuscript. Your suggestions and critiques have made this a much better book.

And thanks to Corey Fowler for being the artist who finally created the cover illustration I wanted. I hope it encourages you, the reader, to sit down at your desk and write a great book for the rest of us to read.

Warning/Disclaimer

Table of Contents

"I was going to write one book and then go back to hair dressing. Now I think...Oakbrook Publishing House could become a million dollar company." — Willie Ripple, stay-at-home mother and author of five books.

"Our creation of new books...and the knowledge that we are creating culinary pleasure for the public that buys our books is more rewarding that anything else we have ever done." — Robert Hoffman. He and his wife, Virginia Hoffman, started a publishing company after they retired.

"The idea that if you write a good book, it will turn into a bestseller is nonsense. Your book may be good, but if the publisher does a bad job, it won't matter. I've got more control over my books now, and that makes them better." — Peter Kent, multi-published author.

"People say you have to have one book, then two books, and then four books, but you don't have to be big in that way." — Barbara Hudgins, divorced mother and travel writer who supports herself with one book.

"My focus is to get unusual sales...[but] you can't bank on these sales because they are very fluky. It's like fishing when you land a great big one out of nowhere. They don't follow any particular rhyme or reason." — Diane Pfeiffer, mother of two children who sells tens of thousands of books as premiums.

"I had a hard time the first few years. People would say, 'Do you want to go out for breakfast?' and I would say, 'Let me check the mail first to see if I got any money.'" Cheri Thurston, former middle school teacher who decided to write and publish the books she wished were available for her classes.

"I'd recommend that authors test market their books online as e-books. It's a brave new world out there and a very exciting time for writers." M.J. Rose, the first self-published author to sell a novel to a major book club.

"I always have to be prepared to lock the door and move somewhere else. I can only pay part-time attention to my job." Bonnie Marlewski-Probart, a woman who has moved ten times during the nine years she's been married.

"Pick a niche and stay with it. It is so much easier to do your marketing once you get a few books that appeal to the same readers." — Connie Shelton, publisher of more than half a dozen mystery authors.

"I thought I would go through the big book distributors and sell my first book through the chains." — Gayle Mitchell, a publisher who sells 90% of her books directly to consumers.

"Unless you are ... a known personality like an actor or politician or rock star, the chances of getting a first book picked up by a publisher are almost non-existent." — Gordon Miller, former executive who focused first on regional success and gained the attention of several New York publishing houses.

"We can take off and do something else regardless of the day of the week or the hour. Now we have to look at our watches to tell what day it is." — Sue Freeman and Rich Freeman, happy corporate dropouts.

Chapter Fourteen
Part-Time Publisher, Full-Time Income..209

"I've owned several businesses, and publishing is by far the easiest one I've tried." — Kenn Amdahl, a publisher who didn't expect a lot of success, but who got it anyway.

Chapter Fifteen
Switching to E-Books 221

"$8.95 is the magic number for e-books. I can offer a 50 page e-book by any author for $5 and nobody buys it. But if I offer a 50 page e-book at $8.95, everybody buys it, depending on the topic, of couse." Angela Adair-Hoy, top-selling e-book author.

Afterword 235

Appendix A
Profiled Publishing Companies 243

Appendix B
Publisher & Writer Associations 247

Appendix C
List Servs 255

Appendix D
Companies and Service Providers 257

Appendix E
Useful Web Sites 265

Foreword

Whether you sell your manuscript to a publisher or publish it yourself, the author must do the promotion. Writing and promoting are completely different challenges. But, one person can successfully be the author, the publisher, the publicist, the shipping person, and the bookkeeper—and end up with a profit. This book proves it.

Suzanne Thomas's newest book, *Make Money Self-Publishing*, describes how fourteen publishers have written, published, and sold enough books to support themselves. You get the inside stories of real people in real life situations. Not only will you learn about their successes, but also about their mistakes. You will discover that you can succeed even if some of your marketing efforts don't produce the results you expected.

Whether you are new to self-publishing or already have several books in print, you will find out how to increase the odds that your publishing company will make money. You will gain insights into how to determine the size of your print runs, how to market your books effectively, what type of income you can expect, and how long it will take before your publishing business can support you.

Perhaps you suspect that successful self-publishers are somehow different, but the publishers in this book are ordinary people. No matter whether you've written a regional or national title, fiction or nonfiction, a cookbook or a textbook, you will find someone here to be your role model.

Instead of reinventing the wheel, you can learn from their experiences. Just like Olympic athletes who visualize themselves performing perfectly, and thereby improve their real-world abilities, so too can you leap ahead in your skill level as a publisher.

Even if you started your publishing company last week, reading *Make Money Self-Publishing* can help you gain years of knowledge, while avoiding costly mistakes. Each of the profiled publishers have faced the same problems you have. Given the limitations of their available time and their budgets, they have figured out the best ways to sell their books. Some sell through traditional outlets such as bookstores while others sell their books in electronic format or through Internet bookstores. You can live through their experiences vicariously, imagining what the results would be for your book.

Though the job of a self-publisher is challenging and satisfying, the day-to-day work can sometimes be discouraging. Along with the successes come setbacks. Perhaps a wholesaler returned a carton of your books. Maybe your sales numbers have started to drop. Or a public relations company hasn't produced results.

At moments like these it is important to have friends who can help with advice, but they aren't always available when you need them. The publishers in this book, however, can act as handy substitutes, conveniently waiting on your bookshelf. What did Cheri Thurston do to reduce returns from wholesalers? How did the Hoffmans rejuvenate the sales of one of their cookbooks after annual sales dropped to 1,000 copies? What did Gayle Mitchell do when she decided she could market her book better than the company she had hired?

Sometimes you won't be looking for solutions to particular problems. Instead you may want an injection of enthusiasm. Re-reading your favorite chapters will inspire you to try something new, remind you of an idea you had forgotten, or motivate you to write the next book. Each chapter is a story, and beyond their educational value, they are also plain fun to read.

Make Money Self-Publishing is a valuable addition to any publisher's library. It's an invaluable reference for any self-publisher who needs encouragement and guidance. Suzanne's book provides you with valuable information sweetened by a huge dose of inspiration. If you want to make money as a publisher, then you should read this book.

—Dan Poynter, *The Self-Publishing Manual.* http:// ParaPub.com

Introduction

Creating a book in physical or electronic format is the main criterion of success for projects such as a family genealogy or a grandparent's memoirs. However, many people would like to make money from their publishing efforts, and not just a little money. They want to earn their livings from writing and publishing. Successful self-publishing for them means more than getting their manuscripts transformed into quality books. They also want to make enough money to support themselves.

Self-publishing is expanding at an incredible rate in the United States. Currently over 7,000 people are expected to start their own publishing houses each year. Yet many of these new publishers will make only small profits or none at all. If they could learn how to run a profitable publishing company from small publishers who have figured out how to do this, then their odds of financial success would be much better.

Make Money Self-Publishing is intended to help people succeed financially while writing, publishing, and selling books. Because people learn more easily through stories rather than from dry how-to instructions, the majority of the chapters in this book focus on in-depth profiles of self-publishers who are making large enough incomes to support themselves by selling their written words.

For example, though you may read somewhere that a good book cover is essential, that advice hits home when you find out what happened to someone's sales when they didn't get this step right. It's easier to remember all the details that lead to publishing success when you learn them through other people's personal experiences.

The real life examples in this book will help you as you make the numerous decisions involved in producing a book. Should you do a hardcover book, or would a paperback version be better? How many books should you print? Where should you sell them? Which marketing ideas would best suit your book and your temperament? Is it a good idea to buy ads in a magazine targeted to radio show producers? Are some book distributors easier to work with than others? Should you try to sell through bookstores, or would gift stores be a better bet for your book?

It's also important to have benchmarks so you can evaluate how you are doing. How long does it take to start making a profit? How many copies do other publishers sell each year? Do their sales for a title decrease or increase each year? Knowing this type of information can be wonderfully reassuring as well as helpful when you make decisions and projections for the future.

The publishers profiled in *Make Money Self-Publishing* share their failures as well as their successes. They also demonstrate how a wide variety of approaches and timetables can all lead to profitable publishing. A few of the publishers followed traditional publishing paths while others headed to the radio airwaves or to the gift stores. Some became almost overnight successes while others built their publishing companies over a number of years.

The publishers themselves are a broad range of people from retirees to corporate dropouts and a divorced mother. Financing ranged from borrowed shoestring budgets to five figure savings accounts. Locations varied from coast to coast as well as places in-between.

Successful book topics for these publishers included the typical non-fiction fare as well as fiction and poetry. Some books are regional in nature while others are aimed at a national or international market. Some publishers have also branched out into publishing books written by other authors.

Make Money Self-Publishing is the book I wanted to read just after I started Gemstone House Publishing. Though I had heard about some of the giant self-publishing successes such as

The Celestine Prophecy or *The Mutant Down Under*, I realized that these books and their authors were making the news precisely because they were so unusual. I needed intermediary level publishing role models, people who, if they were not making a fortune, were at least making a living as self-publishers.

The people in this book have made money with their writing and publishing. They have either cleared a $20,000 annual profit or have sold their book rights for a substantial sum. Many of the profiled publishers are earning incomes well into the five or six figures.

One particularly interesting trend I observed was how many small publishers sell the rights to one or more of their books to larger publishers. I hadn't realized how eager the big publishers are to acquire book rights from self-publishers and small presses. They also pay more for books with proven market appeal than they do for untested manuscripts. So even if your goal is to be published by someone else, self-publishing may be the best way to attract the attention of an editor.

Interviewing these successful self-publishers taught me an incredible amount about publishing. Hopefully you will be able to learn just as much by reading their stories and getting the inside scoop on what it takes to become a profitable publisher.

Small presses are steadily stealing market share from the East Coast publishing houses. No longer do these corporate giants control what Americans read. Books that don't interest East Coast editors are being self-published across the country and are selling thousands of copies. I hope that *Make Money Self-Publishing* will help you to contribute to this beneficial explosion of publishing viewpoints through your own financially successful self-published books.

Chapter One

Self-Publishing 101

Some people self-publish because they decide it is the only way they will ever see their books in print. Others are unwilling to sell their manuscripts to a publisher who may handle them poorly. A few self-publishers know from the start that they want to publish their own work plus perhaps other authors' books as well. And some authors want to be self-publishers only temporarily. They intend to establish the salability of their books so they can sell their publishing rights to New York publishers for far more than most first-time authors can typically obtain.

No matter why self-publishing interests you, reading this book will expose you to ideas you probably haven't considered. You'll be able to peek inside the operations of fourteen micro-publishers to discover how they run their businesses. You'll learn how many books they printed and at what cost, the marketing ideas that worked and the ones that didn't, and how many copies they've sold and at what price. This type of concrete information will give you a starting point for your own business projections. If you've been in the publishing business for a number of years, you'll be able to compare your methods and results and improve them.

The people profiled in the following chapters are earning incomes that range from the modest to the extremely comfortable. Although most of them make good money selling their books, a few qualified for this book by selling their book rights for tens or hundreds of thousands of dollars.

These publishers have approached their businesses in different ways because of their varying personal situations. Having children who need attention or a spouse who frequently relocates has forced some publishers to limit the amount of time they give to their presses. One couple, tired of the corporate rat race, intentionally structured their company, Footprint Press, to allow plenty of time to go hiking. Another couple, bored with retirement, created their company, The Hoffman Press, because they had too much free time on their hands.

Some of the publishers are writers who had problems with the traditional publishing world. One multi-published author, Peter Kent, was unhappy with how his books were being handled. In response he started his own company, Top Floor Publishing. A fiction writer, M.J. Rose, had trouble getting a signed contract for one of her novels until she self-published under the imprint Lady Chatterley's Library.

Gordon Miller recognized that since he was a first time author, he wouldn't get a good offer from a major publisher. He self-published his book and focused on creating a regional best seller. It wasn't long before he attracted the attention of a major publisher, hired a top notch agent to represent him, and eventually signed a $250,000 two-book contract.

Would-be and current publishers can increase their odds of success by learning from the experiences shared by the publishers in this book. What types of books sell the best? Where should they be sold? How many can be sold over what time period? How long does it take for a self-publisher to become self-supporting? What induces a New York publisher to offer a big advance for the rights to a self-published book? What are realistic time lines for achieving various publishing goals? Is it best to start out part-time or full-time?

Reading this book will allow you to take the bits and pieces that most closely match your personal style, your type of book, and your goals, and then use that information to construct or alter your business plan. You may realize that the type of book you want to publish can support you by itself, or else you may discover that you'll need to write at least five books before you can quit your main job. You may decide to select your titles or build your company with an eye to selling them in the future. You may be intrigued by the idea of publishing other authors in addition to yourself.

How to Use This Book

Experienced small publishers may want to skim the rest of this introductory chapter and go straight to the publisher stories. However, if you are reading this book to help you decide whether or not you want to self-publish, you probably are unfamiliar with publishing jargon. This chapter will familiarize you with publishing world basics.

Many of the profiled publishers mention the companies they use from book designers to printers to wholesalers. Contact information for these companies can be found in Appendix D, Companies and Service Providers. Names of regional publishing associations and useful online list serv addresses are provided in Appendix B, Publisher & Writer Associations, and Appendix C, List Servs. Other appendices include recommended books, web sites to visit, e-zines to subscribe to, and contact information for the profiled publishers.

This chapter explains many of the common publishing terms and identifies the dominate industry players, but if you decide to try self-publishing you should also read a detailed how-to book. The top two titles are *The Complete Guide to Self-Publishing* by Tom and Marilyn Ross and *The Self-Publishing Manual* by Dan Poynter. If you want to publish fiction, *Publish Your Novel* by Connie Shelton offers valuable guidance.

The stories in *Make Money Self-Publishing* will give you dozens of marketing ideas, but if you want even more, read *1001 Ways to Sell Your Book* by John Kremer or *Jump Start Your Book Sales* by Tom and Marilyn Ross. You'll have more ideas on how to sell your books than you'll ever have time to use.

How Long Will It Take to Make a Profit?

Like any new business, a publishing company requires an investment of time, energy and money before it begins to generate income for the owner. Anyone who plans to quit a job to start a publishing company should already have a completed manuscript as well as enough funds to print the book and cover living expenses for at least one year. Additional savings or some part-time income is a good idea in case sales don't take off as quickly as hoped. Fiction will take longer than non-fiction to generate a good profit. If you have a background in small business management, marketing or sales, your journey to profitability will be faster because you understand how to get a product sold.

Publishers who have tight budgets or who have little business experience would be wise to start their companies on a part-time basis so they can learn without the financial pressure to make a living quickly from their new venture. It is easy to be overwhelmed as you assimilate the tremendous amount of information required to run a publishing company. If you budget for a longer learning curve, you will have more fun along the way.

You should realize that many self-publishers need 1-2 years to write, edit, typeset and print their first title. Not until the books arrive from the printer will you be able to sell them and earn money (though you may make a few advance sales at a discount). If you sell your title through wholesalers, they will wait to pay you anywhere from 60 to 120 days after they sell your books. Your sales patterns are likely to gyrate in response to an irregular string of marketing successes. It may take months or years before you generate a steady stream of sales and a predictable income.

Where Will You Sell Your Books?

Some publishers sell a large percentage of their books through bookstores. Kenn Amdahl of Clearwater Press has concentrated on getting reviews in printed publications. He has gradually built up a comfortable number of sales through bookstores as buyers read about his books and then ask for them at their local stores.

Peter Kent of Top Floor Publishing and Willie Ripple of Oakbrook Publishing House took a more aggressive position. They rely on a master distributor to get thousands of copies of their titles into hundreds of bookstores quickly.

Other publishers favor non-traditional methods of selling books. Robert and Virginia Hoffman of The Hoffman Press have sold thousands of books to gift stores. Diane Pfieffer of Strawberry Patch has sold her books to gift stores, but she's also sold some of her titles as premiums to large corporations and to a specialty book seller, Reading's Fun. Sue and Rich Freeman of Footprint Press sell through a wide variety of stores such as gas stations and pet stores.

Multiple Titles

Having more than one title makes it far easier to become self-supporting. Much of your overhead remains the same whether you are selling one book or several. If you keep your titles related you can use the same marketing dollars to sell two or three books instead of only one. The income from the sales of multiple titles more easily equals a living wage.

Indeed, one of the major reasons self-publishers with at least five years experience are more likely to earn a living from their writing is because they have had the time to publish more than one title. As they publish new titles, also known as their frontlist, they are still selling their older titles, or their backlist. They are making money off the books they wrote, edited, and typeset two, three, or more years ago.

Publishing multiple titles can be difficult because of the capital requirements. It costs money to print a book, ranging anywhere from $1.50 to $4.00 a copy depending on the size of your print run and if your book has colored illustrations or an unusual format. Because these prices are only a fraction of retail prices, they may sound quite affordable, but you must print your book in substantial quantities in order to get a low print cost.

Even a modest print run of 2,000 copies at a cost of $2.00 apiece will tie up $4,000. This doesn't include what you will have to pay for all the other costs involved in producing a book such as cover design, illustrations, editing, typesetting, and possibly an advance for the author if you didn't write the book yourself.

Therefore, unless you decide to e-publish instead, each book you publish will involve an investment of somewhere between $5,000 and $12,000. Getting five books into print will cost you between $25,000 and $60,000. Few beginning publishers realize how capital intensive this business is, but they quickly learn that their company's growth will be limited more by available funds rather than by a lack of solid book ideas.

If you eventually grow from being a self-publisher into a small press, you will face difficult decisions about your list. You may not be able to afford to keep all of your titles in print. For a clearer look at this dilemma, see Chapter Seven, Success on a Shoestring, or Chapter Ten, Daring to Publish Mysteries.

Some publishers avoid the cost of printing books by publishing e-books instead. Angela Adair-Hoy sells over $48,000 worth of books each year through her two web sites without the expense of printing books. M.J. Rose developed demand for her fiction title online before she committed to printing the book.

Who Gets the Money

Many new self-publishers fail to understand the economics of book publishing. When they discover that books can be printed for a couple of dollars, they conclude that books sell for too much at the local bookstores. They decide to price their books more competitively so they can sell more copies. Then, too late, they discover the hidden costs involved in producing, marketing, and shipping books.

Small publishers don't do well trying to compete against the big publishers on price. For example, you may want to target a niche market too small or specialized to attract the big publishers. This means that your print runs will be smaller and therefore more expensive per book.

Or maybe you decide to publish a national book. This may allow you to save money by doing a bigger print run, but you'll also be competing against the big publishers. This means you'll spend more money per book on marketing. You may have to hire gift reps, travel for book signings and seminars, or send out promotional kits to reporters across the country. To understand more clearly why you should be careful not to underprice, let's look at some of the expenses you'll have as a publisher.

Discounts

Bookstores expect a 40% discount. The stores need this discount to cover the cost of their overhead such as staff, store rent, book shelves, electricity, office supplies, personal property taxes and hopefully have something left over called profit. This 40% discount may seem bad enough, but generally you won't be selling directly to hundreds of different bookstores. Rather you will sell to one or two main wholesalers who will expect a 50-55% discount.

Wholesalers receive this larger discount because they handle the shipping and packing, and because they need to cover their own overhead expenses. Bookstores like to work with wholesalers because they enjoy the convenience of ordering hundreds of books from only one vendor instead of from hundreds of publishers. They get better discounts and simplify their accounting and inventory work.

Gift stores will expect a 50% discount, although unlike the wholesalers they expect to pay shipping costs. If you use reps to sell your title to the gift stores, you'll have to pay the reps a percentage of your book's wholesale price. Your total discount expense when selling to gift stores may end up being 60-65% of your retail price.

Returns

Bookstores and the wholesalers or distributors who sell to the bookstores generally expect the right to return books if they don't sell. This means you are actually selling your books on a consignment basis. When you receive returns, you have wasted the postage you paid to send out the books in the first place. In addition, sometimes the returned books will be damaged. Unless you are willing to risk losing your sales accounts by refusing to issue a credit for these books, you will have to bear the cost of this lost inventory.

Returns can also cause you to overprint a particular title. Your first print run, let's say for 2,500 copies, sells out so you order a second printing of the same size. The day the shipment of new books arrives could turn out to be the same day your wholesaler returns 500 copies from the first printing. Oops. You now have more money tied up in inventory than you had planned. Plus you will have to credit your wholesaler for the returned copies, thereby reducing the size of the check you expected to receive from the wholesaler next month.

Return rates for the industry can approach startling levels. According to the 1998 Romstat report (produced for romance authors by the Romance Writers of America), 1997 hardcover returns were 36.3% and mass market returns equaled 46.4% of shipped copies.

These return rates, however, are for publishers powerful enough to get hundreds of bookstores and other outlets to stock multiple copies of a title. They budget for a certain number of returns and save money on their printing costs by running large print runs.

As a small publisher you probably can't afford to print 25,000 copies. On the other hand, your return rate will be much smaller, most likely under 10%. Many stores won't order your book without a special order in hand unless your title is regional and therefore almost guaranteed to sell to locals and tourists. You won't have the opportunity to flood the market, and this is the good side to the small publisher's struggle to get a title into stores.

It may seem like a goal of zero returns would be best, but that means you are being too cautious. Books won't sell unless buyers can find them. Though some stores won't sell as many copies as you persuade them to stock, other stores will do much better. You won't know which is which unless you try.

The tremendous advantage of selling to any store that isn't a bookstore is you can eliminate the returns problem. When a book is sold to gift stores, for example, it stays sold. You won't get additional orders unless the stores are successful with your title, but at least you'll have the comfort of knowing that these sales are final. This makes projecting your cash flow and printing needs much more accurate.

You can also insist on selling on a prepaid, non-returnable basis. This policy limits the distribution of your book, and will most likely result in lower sales, but it also gives you control over your finances. Depending on the type of book you publish and the way you market it, this policy could work the best for you.

Direct Mail

To sell to consumers through direct mail, you will need money to pay for the mailing pieces. Your direct mail package could include the offer letter, an order sheet and self-addressed envelope, postage, and the rental fee for a mailing list. Because direct mail response rates tend to be low, generally around 2%, the price of your book may not be high enough to justify the expense of a direct mail campaign.

Editing and Typesetting

Typesetting, or laying out, your manuscript can be done on your own computer or be hired out to a freelancer. Paying some-one else costs money, but so does owning a computer and the necessary software. Programs such as Microsoft Word can do an adequate job, but in order to produce the best looking book pos-sible you will have to use a desktop publishing program such as Pagemaker, Framemaker, or Quark.

Covers

You will need to get a top notch cover done for your book. The importance of your cover cannot be overstated. It must be professional and appropriate for your subject. The title must be readable at a distance and the overall impression of the cover should remain good when it's reduced to 2X3 inches for a flyer or an online bookstore's web page.

Cover designers generally charge from $500 to $2,500. If you want to do a color proof to check that the colors you see on your designer's computer screen are what you'll get on your printed book, expect to pay another $100 to $200. Finally, you will have to pay an independent service bureau to do the cover films for you, or pay the printer to do them for you as part of your printing costs.

Storage and Fulfillment

When you print your books, you'll have to pay to have them shipped either to you or to a fulfillment house. On top of the shipping costs, if you don't have room to store your books in your garage or spare bedroom, you'll have to pay for space in a warehouse, rent a storage shed, or pay a fulfillment company to store your books.

You'll also need to insure your books to protect them against damage while you are waiting to sell them. Both your storage and insurance costs will start to add up over time. If you can save $.15 per book by printing an extra 1,000 copies, but it will take you an additional year to sell your inventory at a cost of $.20 per book for storage and insurance, you may discover that it is actually cheaper in the end to do a smaller print run. By printing fewer books you also reduce the amount of capital tied up in inventory as well as the risk of printing more copies than you can sell.

Book wholesalers generally demand that small publishers pay to ship their books to the wholesaler. Unless you hire a fulfillment house, then in addition to postage or freight fees you will need to purchase shipping materials. If you sell directly to bookstores you may be able to charge them shipping. Most gift stores will expect to be charged for shipping, although during slow seasons you may decide to throw in shipping for free as an incentive to buy books then.

Review Copies & Press Kits

You will give away a certain percentage of your books. Reviewers, for example, expect free copies. If you want to be booked as a guest on radio shows, many producers and hosts will expect you to send them review copies as well as additional copies to give away to listeners.

When you send out press kits, you'll have to pay for postage plus the contents of the kits. A press kit may use several sheets of special and expensive paper, a photo of you, a picture of the book cover, and the folder itself. If each press kit costs you $5 in materials, then sending out 200 press kits will cost you $1,000.

If this sounds expensive, add the expense of someone's time to contact the print reviewers and radio station producers, compile and send out the kits, and track the results. While it's common for people to refer to publicity as being free, it's not. However, it does provide the biggest bang for the buck in most situations.

Telephone

A business phone line costs more than a personal phone line, but if you have children who may not answer professionally or a spouse who doesn't want to take calls for your publishing company, getting a separate business number is probably best. If you are planning on doing radio interviews over the telephone, you can avoid the cost of call waiting. It's not professional to have the line beeping when someone is interviewing you for radio.

You will need either voice mail, an answering machine, or an answering service to take messages. It is possible in some areas of the country to get a voice mail service that allows callers to choose different voice boxes depending on whether they want to place an order or leave a message for the staff. Retail customers can be given a detailed message telling them how to place an order while wholesalers and radio producers can go directly to the marketing mailbox. If you can only have one message on your system, then keep your message as short as possible.

If you hire an answering service, you will need to train them on how you want your calls answered. You'll also need to forward calls to them from your phone whenever you won't be available to answer the phone and remember to check for messages later. Bonnie Makowski-Probart of K & B Products found that an answering service worked best for her company for a number of years.

Credit Card Expenses

If you want to be able to accept credit cards, you will have to get merchant status. Various programs exist for small businesses, but you will pay monthly fees, share a percentage of your sales, and may have to buy or rent a credit card terminal. Unless you plan on selling a number of your books directly to consumers, either at seminars, through direct mail, or on a secure web site, you may discover that your credit card expenses eat up all your profits from the additional sales.

Travel

A small publisher will travel for many reasons. You may attend publishers' conferences, go out of state for book signings, act as your own rep to gift stores and bookstores, or visit acquisition librarians at major libraries. You may also travel to different cities for television or radio appearances. Sometimes a show will pay for your hotel room or airfare, but it's rare for the smaller shows to cover all your expenses. Some costs will end up coming out of your pocket.

Publisher's Liability Insurance

Depending on your book's subject matter, you may want to purchase publisher's insurance. Americans are a litigious people, and someone could decide to sue you. Depending on risk factors such as your topic, exactly what you say in your book, and how many copies you sell per year, insurance costs can run $.50 per book or higher.

Web Site

Even if you design and maintain your own web site, you will have to pay a monthly hosting charge. Don't assume that the mere existence of a web site will cause orders for your book to pour in. Unless you are willing to market your web site by publishing an e-magazine like Peter Kent or Angela Adair-Hoy, you may not get enough sales to cover your expenses.

Even if you don't make a ton of sales off your web site, having one can still be valuable because of the more substantial image it gives to your press. It can serve as an ancillary marketing piece for traditional promotional efforts. It gives you the opportunity to deliver updates to readers, and it provides a place to post submission guidelines to potential authors.

Print Runs

Deciding on the size of your print run can be very tricky. The more books you print, the cheaper your cost per book. This potential for increasing your profit margins can become a strong motivation after you subtract all of your expenses from your retail sales price and see what is left. Every dime you save on the printing is another dime you make.

But large print runs come with the risk that you won't be able to sell all of the books. You also need to ship, store, and insure them. Sometimes you simply can't afford a large print run because you don't have the necessary capital.

The rough rule of thumb is to print only as many books as you can sell in two years. This rule isn't very useful for a first time publisher or an established publisher who's trying a book in a brand new area. Without a track record, how can you know how many books you'll sell in two years?

You could try to find out the print runs of other small publishers who have books in the same field as your book. You can find these publishers through publisher associations and on list servs. Remember to ask them if any special factors helped or hurt their sales, and try to look at a copy of their books so you can compare the quality and price against the book you intend to produce.

Failing all else, start small. Do a print run of only 500 to 1,000 copies. If the book sells poorly, you'll have less money at risk. If the book sells well, you'll have lost a bit of profit, but you'll have a much better feel for how big your second print run should be. You'll also have the opportunity to add glowing reviews to your cover. Kenn Amdahl of Clearwater Press thinks this opportunity to add positive quotes to your book is the best reason to keep the initial print run modest.

Publisher Associations and List Servs

Numerous publisher associations exist on the local, regional, and national levels. Networking with your colleagues can keep you motivated, prevent you from feeling isolated, give you great marketing ideas, answer your questions, and save you money. Most associations have modest annual membership fees ranging from $40 to $100 per year. Conferences can be local and cost around $100, or you can attend more expensive national conferences.

You'll want to join a few publishing associations both for the educational opportunities and for access to special group benefits such as reduced shipping costs, discounts on items from car rentals to software programs, and help getting credit card merchant status. A list of associations is provided in Appendix B.

List servs give you an online community of fellow publishers and would-be publishers to answer your questions and share recommendations. List servs are online discussion groups where people who are interested in the same topics can ask and answer questions. Joining a publishers list serv gives you a place to ask for references on wholesalers and printers, find out where to get the best prices for items such as padded envelopes and packing tapes, and anything else that a small publisher needs to know. Unlike attending meetings and conferences, you can go online when it's convenient for your schedule. Information on how to subscribe to various publisher and writer list servs is in Appendix C.

Dealing with Distributors and Wholesalers

If you want to do a substantial amount of business with bookstores, you'll need to work either with an exclusive distributor or directly with wholesalers. An exclusive distributor handles all sales to bookstores and wholesalers for you, but will charge up to a 70% discount off the retail price of your book. In exchange the distributor is supposed to market your book directly to the bookstores instead of being merely an order taker. A good distributor can move a lot of books fast while freeing up your time. A bad distributor will take their big discount, but not get your book into the bookstores.

Even if you want to hire an exclusive distributor, you may have trouble getting them to accept your books until after you have established a track record. Instead, you will have to work directly with a number of wholesalers, giving them a discount ranging from 50% to 55%. These wholesalers may include your books in their catalogs or put a flyer advertising your titles in their shipments to bookstores, but generally they won't send reps to bookstores to promote your books. Their main role is to fill orders from libraries and bookstores. You will have to generate the demand that fuels those orders.

Working with Chain Bookstores

Barnes & Noble has over 500 stores. Borders Books and Music has over 200 stores. The smaller chains, B. Dalton and Waldenbooks, have hundreds of additional stores. It's tempting to start calculating how many books you could sell if your titles were stocked in each bookstore, but that's not the way it works. Unless you have a national distributor or a history of books that sell well like Peter Kent of Top Floor Publishing, you may have trouble getting your title accepted by each chain's national buyer for your category.

If the buyer does decide to take a chance, your book may be stocked in just a few of their stores that have strong sales histories for that category. Also, even though Barnes & Noble owns B. Dalton and Borders owns Waldenbooks, these chains have their own buyers. You must approach each buyer separately.

You can start your campaign to get into the national bookstore chains by sending them galley copies of your book. A galley is a copy of the final manuscript, preferably already typeset into its final form, which is sent out before the book is printed. Call each chain's headquarters and ask who the buyer is for your category, and then send that person a galley.

Include information about the author such as previous books by that author, marketing plans for the book and the publicity budget, the size of the first print run, and the cover price. Obviously, chain store buyers will be more interested in a book by an established author with well-funded publicity and marketing efforts and a realistic retail price.

Even if a national buyer for a chain turns you down, the local managers of the chain stores may order a few copies if you inform them of your publicity efforts in their cities. Tell them about newspaper articles, radio appearances, and TV spots. They want to carry the books that their customers want to buy. If you convince them that you'll create demand, they'll give you an order.

As you obtain publicity for your book you should update the chains' buyers. For example, if you are taped for a cable show that will be broadcast in over 100 markets across the country, get a list of those markets, the stations' channels, and their subscriber counts. Even if the national buyers have only stocked you in a few stores, detailed information like this may convince them to add your book to the inventory of additional stores.

If your book has been accepted by Barnes & Noble, you can track sales by calling the Small Press person at the Barnes & Noble headquarters who is assigned to your publishing company. This person can tell you approximately how many of their stores stock your book, how many copies are currently in stock, and how many copies have been sold over a given time period.

End Caps and Display Tables

The chains sell special display space in their stores to publishers. This space is on tables or the displays called end caps at the end of each row of bookcases. These spaces are occasionally available on a regional basis, but generally they are sold by the month for all of the stores.

It's not up to you to decide that you would like to purchase a bit of this prime display space. Usually you have to be invited to participate. Why? Because even though the stores charge a publisher between $2,000 to $3,000 to have a book displayed on end caps or a table, the stores also want to make money by having the book sell extra copies. Your book must already be stocked nationwide in a particular bookstore chain, plus the buyer for your category must believe your book is one that will benefit from this special exposure.

If you are offered the opportunity to have your book get special display space, ask for a small press discount. It may save you hundreds of dollars.

Sometimes you can get your book on an end cap or table for free if you let a manager know you are a local author and your book fits the theme of one of the display spaces, say investing or outdoor sports. Doing a book signing also will get you prime display space for a short period of time before the signing.

Book Signings

You can ask managers of chain bookstores to let you do book signings. They often say yes even if the chain's buyer for your categaory hasn't accepted your book. The managers will special order copies for the signing through one of your wholesalers or directly from you.

Book signings do better if you combine them with a slide presentation or a short lecture about your topic. You also shouldn't rely on the store to attract attendees. It's up to you to send out publicity releases before the event, get listed in newspapers' calendars of events, and notify the TV stations. Ask the store for its list of local media. You may not want to send out a full-fledged press kit to everyone, but send them something and tell them how they can request a free review copy of the book.

If you are going out of state and want to set up book signings with Barnes & Noble, you can get the addresses for their stores by going to their online bookstore,bn.com. On their home page you can select the store locator button. The next page will invite you to enter either a city and state or zip code, and you'll get the phone numbers and addresses of the closest stores. If you want only the bigger stores, you can request to be shown only stores that sell music or have a cafe.

Bear in mind that this database of stores may not be kept completely up to date. The same goes for phone directories. If you are having trouble locating a store that wants a book signing event on the day you'll be in town, ask about new stores that may not yet be listed. The customer relation managers at Barnes & Noble stores and the community relations coordinators at Borders Books and Music stores talk to each other. They know who is completely booked with events and who is looking to fill a few blank spots.

Some book signing times are more difficult to book. November and early December are popular because of the multitude of holiday shoppers. Although normally you will be successful scheduling book signings by calling the stores two to three months in advance, you should extend this to four to five months for signings during the holiday season.

Sales from book signings occur before, during, and after the event itself. Depending on the size of the store and whether or not the event is advertised, the manager will probably consider it a successful signing if 15-25 books sell. Because many of the big chain stores only advertise book signings in their monthly store newsletter, try to schedule your signings toward the end of the month. That way more shoppers who visit the store will have a chance to pick up that month's newsletter and learn about your upcoming appearance.

Book signings can be time consuming and don't work well for every book. Unless you get publicity for each event, you will sometimes have a poor turnout. If you have to travel out of state to do a signing, your immediate expenses may exceed the income from the additional sales.

On the positive side, signings can get your book stocked by stores that previously didn't offer it. If you are going to be visiting a city anyway, scheduling a signing while you are there can provide a deadline to prod the media into giving you or your book some coverage. It can also allow you to deduct some of your trip as a business expense.

Doing signings also gives you the opportunity to talk with your book's readers directly. You will learn what they most want to know as well as how your book could be improved in its next edition. You can also ask the attendees who like your book to post positive reviews at the online bookstores. Online shoppers and reporters doing research like to see lots of reviews, and prefer some of them to be recent. If all of your reviews are old, your book could appear to be out of date.

Online Bookstores

Amazon.com prides itself on offering every title it can. Whether or not you submit your book to them, it will probably be offered on their web site as long as you have submitted your book's vital statistics to R.R. Bowker's *Books in Print*. You can set your own terms with Amazon.com, but unless you become an Advantage member, your book may be listed in a way that discourages sales. Customers don't like being told they'll have to wait 4-6 weeks for a book to be shipped.

The better option for most small publishers is to join Amazon.com's Advantage program. You will have to give Amazon.com a 55% discount off the retail price of your book and pay shipping costs. In exchange, they will stock your book and list it as available to ship within 24 hours. This quick availability has a dramatic effect on sales, and can justify the larger-than-normal bookstore discount for online stores.

Many publishers love to watch their books' sales rankings. Amazon.com lists each book by its sale numbers against every other book, and they also rank them by category. As in golf, the goal is to have a low number.

The sales rankings can be important for several reasons. Consumers may use them to judge the popularity of a book. Book club editors can look at them to get a rough idea of the salability of a book. And bookstore managers may check these numbers before deciding to carry a book in their bricks and mortar store.

Book Clubs

A sale to a book club can equal thousands of copies, but you won't make a lot of money. While smaller clubs may buy copies directly from you as the publisher, the larger clubs will want to print their own copies. They will pay you, the publisher, a royalty based on the discounted club price for the book. Despite the low profit per book, the exposure can be tremendous.

Galleys can be sent to the book clubs before your book is printed. If you are lucky, you'll catch their interest and be able to add the words "Book Club Selection" to your cover. Even if you don't sell your book to a club when it's brand new, they may pick it up later. Erika Tsang of Doubleday Book Club was looking at fiction titles on Amazon.com when she saw all the rave reviews for M.J. Rose's novel. She asked for a review copy, liked it, and made it an alternate selection, the first self-published novel ever picked up by a national book club.

To increase your chances of having your book picked up after it's published, you should update the book clubs with your sales figures. If your title starts to sell in the thousands, the editor may decide to take a second look at it. Let them know whenever something noteworthy happens. Polite persistence can lead to a book club deal.

Selling to Libraries

Some wholesalers are known for their library sales. Quality Books sells exclusively to libraries while Baker & Taylor sells to both libraries and bookstores. To get your non-fiction book carried by Quality (they don't handle fiction), you should either send a review copy or galley to their Title Selection Committee. Along with your book, you must include the Quality book information form. If they accept your book, they'll have their reps present it to acquisition librarians across the country.

Because the reps physically can't carry hundreds of different books with them as they travel, you'll need to provide 30 extra copies of your book cover or Quality will charge you to make the copies. Quality lets its publishers know on a monthly basis how many copies of their books have sold.

Baker & Taylor charges $125 to list a title in their title database, but they will waive this fee for members of Publishers Marketing Association (PMA) or the Small Publishers Association of North America (SPAN). This fee waiver may come with contingencies such as participating in a marketing mailing, so check on what is required.

On the other hand, if Baker & Taylor start to get orders for your book, they will approach you and ask to carry your book. They will waive their fee in this situation because they know they can sell copies. Just make sure you are listed in R.R. Bowker's *Books in Print* so Baker & Taylor can find you.

Even if your book is carried by one or more of the library wholesalers, you should still try to create demand for it. Because librarians pay attention to good reviews in magazines such as *Library Journal, Publishers Weekly, Kirkus Reviews*, or *Booklist,* you should definitely send galleys to these publications. You must send galleys at least 3-4 months in advance of your book's publication date because these review magazines will not look at already published books.

If none of these magazines review your book, or if your book is already in print, the next best approach is to find a librarian who will write a good review for you and give you permission to quote that review in a flyer.

You can rent mailing lists of libraries, photocopy lists of libraries out of a directory at your largest local library, or find addresses for libraries online. Send the flyer to the attention of the acquisition librarian for your category whether non-fiction, fiction or children's. If you want to save some money, you can join in a co-op mailing instead of sending out your flyers independently.

PMA offers library co-op mailings to its members. Your flyer is included in a packet with numerous other flyers. But if you think your flyer will get lost in a large mailing, you could choose to join up with other publishers for a private co-op mailing.

These private mailings typically limit the number of flyers enclosed in an envelope. Usually only three flyers are sent together by first class instead of bulk mail rate. You can learn about these mailings by joining one of the online publisher list servs, through your local publishing association, or by organizing a co-op mailing yourself.

Librarians in your home state will be the most open to carrying your book. Many of them feel that buying the books written by local authors is part of their mission. You can meet these librarians by stopping in at libraries and asking to speak with the appropriate acquisition librarian. Or you can attend the annual library conference for your state. Your local publishing association may have a booth there for their members' books, or one of your wholesalers such as Quality may display your book for you for a small fee.

Some publishers fear that having their books in libraries will cause them to lose sales. They believe a consumer won't buy a book if it's available for free. If your book is a stand-alone novel (not part of a series), this could be a valid concern. Most readers only want to read a story once. However, if your title is non-fiction, readers may decide they want their own reference copy at home. Be sure to include ordering instructions at the back of your book so it's easy for them to order a copy from you.

If your fiction book is part of a series, a reader may want to read all the related books. If that reader's library doesn't have them, you will receive an order or the local bookstore will make a sale. And even if a reader doesn't want to buy a copy of a novel for herself, she may decide to buy a copy of a book she liked to give away as a gift.

Radio Interviews

Some books can be sold effectively by the author appearing as a guest on radio programs. Guest spots can be obtained the hard, slow way by calling producers individually and asking them to book you as a guest. The easier way to get booked for shows it to place an ad in an industry magazine such as *Radio-TV Interview Report* or on web sites such as GuestFinders.com. Producers look at the ads for potential guests and call the ones who interest them.

While these ads cost several hundreds of dollars, that expense has to be weighed against the hourly cost of having someone call the producers directly. Paying for an ad so they call you may actually be more cost effective. Once you get on a show, you may be invited back for repeat appearances.

Each time you appear on a radio show, you should take the time to either listen to a recording of the program or later review with yourself the questions the host asked. Could you have made your answers tighter? Clearer? More amusing? Soon you'll be able to identify the questions that reappear consistently. Make sure you practice your answers to these questions until you can convey exactly the type of response you want.

Hardcovers Versus Paperbacks

Based on the sales experience of Gemstone House Publishing, librarians do prefer hardcover books over paperbacks, but only if they get a higher quality book. Given the choice between a Smyth sewn hardcover and a trade paperback version, librarians prefer the Smyth sewn. But if the hardcover is glued instead of sewn, the librarians will favor the cheaper paperback.

Consumers, if given the choice of the same title in two versions, will generally select the hardcover about 20% of the time. At Christmas the percentage may exceed 50% because people like to give hardcovers as gifts. The brick and mortar bookstores tend to order only the trade paperback version, so consumers will only be presented with the hardcover option by online bookstores.

If you do a split run when you print your books, meaning you bind some copies as hardcover and some as paperback, you will face the tricky decision of what proportion of books to bind one way or the other. If you have too many of either version, you will instantly make some books obsolete if you want to update your book when you reprint the version that has sold out. Also your sales ranking on Amazon.com, a reference source for many journalists and librarians, will not look as good as it could for each version because the sales for each version will be ranked separately instead of being combined for a better ranking.

To avoid these problems, many publishers come out with the hardcover version first and switch to paperback when they reprint. Reference titles and those that make good gifts tend to do better in hardcover than other books, but for most books the safest bet financially is to produce a paperback book. A lower price point reduces your publishing risk, and libraries will buy your book if they want it even if it's not available in hardcover.

Ready, Set, Go!

Now that you are familiar with the basic jargon of the publishing business, you're ready to move on to the publisher stories. If you have trouble with any of the terms you encounter, flip back to this chapter for help or look in the index to get page numbers.

So much information is packed into the following self-publisher chapters that it may be difficult to absorb everything in one reading. So relax instead, and let it soak in slowly. You can always read a chapter a second time, or look up sections when you need to review information about a particular topic.

Even as you gain experience as a publisher, re-reading this book will be valuable to you. Different parts of the stories will become more meaningful. You'll notice marketing ideas you have yet to try, and be reassured that your troubles along the way have been shared by other successful small presses. Hopefully, too, this book will give you a renewed jolt of enthusiasm if you occasionally find yourself wondering why you became a publisher. You'll be reminded that although this business comes with its challenges, it can also provide an intensely satisfying way to make a living.

Chapter Two

School Party Volunteer

Willie Ripple never meant to become a publisher. A hairdresser by training, she took time out to have three children. One fateful day after her oldest entered kindergarten, he brought home a paper asking if anyone wanted to help with the school parties. "I had always loved parties," Willie says. "I called and said, 'Ooh, I would love to be this head room parent; what does that mean?' The room parent chairperson was so excited. She said, 'Oh my goodness, we don't usually get enthusiastic calls like this.'"

When Willie went to the orientation meeting, a mother from another kindergarten class brought in a pile of books to share as sources for party ideas. "She showed us a book with some cute games we could do, and a holiday book with a little piece of a Halloween thing, and yet another book with a neat idea."

Willie thought the lady was nuts for combing through all these different books. Why not get one school party book and be done with it?

"So I went to the library and told the librarian I needed a book on school parties. She said there wasn't a book like that, but I asked her to please check. She did, and the book wasn't there. I said, 'No big deal, I'll go to the bookstore and buy it.' When I didn't see anything on the shelves, I told the clerk how I had volunteered to do the school party for my son's class. I needed the book that told me how to do it. But she'd never seen a book like that either.

"I was floored. I went back to the library thinking I would be like the lady whose approach I had laughed at, gathering all these books and trying to piece ideas together. Fortunately, my mom had done a lot of really cool parties. I think I got the creative edge from her."

Willie proceeded to be head room parent for each of her three kids even if that meant doing three parties in one afternoon. "I juggled. Other parents helped me, and I ran back and forth between the rooms. Over the years my parties became more and more creative, until finally five people came up to me in one week and said I should write a book.

"It was the weirdest thing. It started with a kindergarten teacher. I remember standing there and she said, 'Willie, you have to write a book.' 'A book about what?' I asked. 'Parties,' she said. 'Because your parties are the most organized, creative and fun I've seen in fifteen years of teaching.'

"I decided to write a book about Halloween and Valentine's Day school parties with a little section about teacher gifts tucked in at the back. I wasn't expecting to start a publishing company. I thought I would sell some copies of my first and only book, and then go back to hairdressing."

Willie wasn't sure how to write her book, so off she went to the bookstore to buy a book to help her figure out what to do. "When I flipped open Dan Poynter's book on self-publishing, one of the first things it said was, 'You have decided to write a book and you don't know what to do.' And I'm like, yes! This is me!

"He said to pretend I was sitting across from somebody and then try to explain something to them. So I sat there at my table pretending that someone was listening to me. I would say out loud, 'To do this game you need this and this.' Then I would write it down. I still use this process today for each new book I write."

Writing and Producing the Book

It took Willie two years to get the book to the printers. "I wrote the book in paragraph form, including the lists of supplies. It was hard to read, but I didn't know what to do to fix it so I contacted some freelance editors."

The first editor was a man with no kids, the second was a grandma whom Willie thought was kind of old-fashioned, and the third editor was an active mom. "She planned school parties at her daughter's school, so she'd gone through the same experiences," Willie says. "She was a parent, and she understood."

When Willie explained that she didn't know how to handle the format of her book, her editor asked her to show her a book she did like. "I showed her a book that had step-by-step directions. She thought that was what parents would like best, so we used that format."

As Willie kept writing it became apparent that she had enough material for two books, one for Halloween and another for Valentine's Day. She decided to write the Halloween book first. "I just hated the editing stage," Willie admits. "The manuscript kept coming back. Edit after edit I'd have to rephrase a sentence and then my editor and even my husband would critique it again."

Willie wanted her book to have illustrations. When she had originally decided to write a school party book, she had tried to co-write it with a neighbor. That hadn't worked, but the woman's daughter, Heather, was an artist. "Heather showed me this witch she had drawn on one of her sketch pads, and I just loved it. It was so cute that I decided to hire her to do the illustrations.

"I ended up paying Heather $500. I also gave her twelve books and the option of buying more at a discounted price. She illustrated the Halloween books, both of the Valentine books, and she'll also do the illustrations for the Christmas book and slumber party book. She's great, though not your everyday kind of person; she's an artist."

When Willie was ready to layout the book she looked through the yellow pages for a graphic designer. "I wanted someone located close to me because after seeing the editor every couple of days, I realized I didn't want to drive too far."

Working with her designer to decide how to do the layout challenged Willie because the book consisted of many sets of instructions with corresponding illustrations. "It was hard, a lot of decisions, and I didn't know what I wanted. He had great ideas on designing the whole book and how to tie everything together."

Willie had hoped to have Heather do the cover artwork for the Halloween book, but her drawing didn't feel right to Willie. She wanted something different. "I had joined PMA and CIPA (Colorado Independent Publishers Association). I called some of the cover designers who advertised in their publications, and they told me a cover would cost $1,000 to $1,500. I thought, are you kidding me? I never realized they cost so much."

Eventually she contacted Bobbie Shupe with E.P. Puffin & Company. "Cover designers from other companies had been talking with me, but I didn't get good vibes. When Bobbie came to the house she showed me some of the book covers she had designed for other CIPA members, and I thought they looked like what I wanted."

Willie was clear on what elements should be included in the cover illustration for her first book. "There are eight themes in the Halloween book and I wanted all eight incorporated in the illustration: bat, cat, Frankenstein, ghost, pumpkin, skeleton, spider, and witch. I also wanted a schoolhouse."

She found the perfect model schoolhouse when her family went to Steamboat Springs for a baseball tournament. "Right before you get into town there is this little beat-up, red schoolhouse with the mountains behind it. I thought it was so cute." The schoolhouse later appeared on the Valentine books as well, providing continuity between the covers of Willie's first three books.

Many people advised Willie not to include the word "school" in her title. They thought she could sell more copies if she didn't restrict her book to school parties. "But I knew I was filling a niche. I remembered how I felt when the bookstore clerk told me there wasn't a school Halloween party book; my heart just sank. I didn't care about selling more copies. The whole idea was to write this book to help parents like me."

Winning the Benjamin Franklin Award

Willie entered *Halloween School Parties...What Do I Do?*® in the annual Benjamin Franklin Award sponsored by PMA and won two first place awards, one for cover design using three or more colors, and the other one for best first book from a new publisher. "After winning the award we noticed an increase in sales that year. It made some of the bookstores take a look. Actually, right after we got home from the PMA show I got a letter from Marcella Smith at the Barnes & Noble small press department in New York. They had reviewed my book and wanted to carry it when I got a distributor."

Willie also entered her first two books in the CIPA book awards. They each took second place. "Placing in that contest didn't have the same impact as winning the Benjamin Franklin awards, but the stickers were nice to put on the covers of the books. Plus people were impressed when I told them I had won several awards. Getting awards helps sales."

In terms of entering contests for feedback, Willie hasn't received a lot of useful comments. "Critique sheets would have blanks specified for comment, but the judges rarely filled them in. One guy did say he thought the little red school house on the cover of *Valentine School Parties...What Do I Do?*® was smarmy, that even teachers would turn up their noses at it. Other judges would write that they didn't know if something was okay for my market, and I wondered why they were judges if they didn't know stuff like that."

Special Problems with Seasonal Books

Each of Willie's current books have a season, and if her books aren't in the stores at the right time, she has to wait a year for the next chance to sell them. "Our distributor, IPG (Independent Publishing Group), sold out their copies of *Valentine School Parties...What Do I Do?*® in December, then called us in early January, 1999, to ask us if we had any more books. We did, and we shipped them out. IPG got them around January 10th, but when I went to the bookstores to check they said there were no copies available for them to buy. I called Ingram, and they didn't have any books."

Eventually she discovered that the books were sitting in IPG's warehouse waiting to be released. "It was a mistake on their part. The books should have been released, but instead they had been sitting there for two weeks. The operations manager at IPG told me he was releasing them, and he would overnight them to Ingram."

Despite his prompt reaction Willie thought she was still going to have a problem. "Would Ingram realize it was a holiday book and that they should hurry to get them out? Then at the bookstores, would the staff shelve our books quickly instead of letting them sit in the back rooms for awhile? We couldn't control any of this."

As a result of the time it took for the books to move through the distribution network, a lot of books were returned because they didn't hit the shelves in time. "We paid a 10% restocking fee to our distributor," Willie explains. "We didn't feel we should pay all of it because it was their fault for not getting the books out fast enough. They never did rebate us any money, but they did promise to move the books out faster the next time."

For her company's next season, Halloween, Willie made sure to ship the books early. To get them processed quickly at the IPG warehouse she put Halloween stickers on each case of books and wrapped a big sign on top of the pallet along with packages of candy for the warehouse workers. "The sign said, 'I'm a Halloween book, open me instantly.' When I called IPG and asked if they had received my books, they thanked me for the candy and told me they had got the books right out the door."

Willie says IPG has gotten better about ordering early and then getting her books out of the warehouse quickly. "I think they are aware of the situation now. Selling seasonal books can be hard because we're relying on the printer to drop ship the books to IPG on time, then for IPG to get them out of the warehouse, the wholesaler to ship them to the bookstores, and the store employees to shelve the books.

"I can't entirely get away from seasonal books because of the kind of books that fit my What Do I Do® series," Willie says. "My next book is *Christmas Parties...What Do I Do®*, so that's seasonal, too. But the one after that is *Slumber Parties...What Do I Do®*. When that comes out it will sell year round.

"Even without the slumber party book, this next year we'll have books for Halloween, Valentine's Day, and Christmas. We'll cover three different seasons which is nice in terms of paying for the printing, shipping and marketing. Our income will be more balanced."

The Time Crunch

Like many self-publishers who want to publish numerous books, Willie quickly found herself squeezed for time. "I have all these great marketing and book ideas, but who has time to do them? I'm in my office two to four hours a day answering the phones and e-mails, packaging the books, and opening the regular mail, the basic day-to-day stuff to keep the company running and my desk clear."

Willie's daily schedule starts with getting the kids off to school, then exercising, picking up the house, and doing the daily stuff. Then her kids are back home before she can tackle the big projects. "I'll have errands to run with the kids, and almost every single night we have some event for them. There's no time for me to write except late at night."

Willie has tried having employees. "It's a struggle because we're not big enough to really afford a full-time assistant, but we need help so I can write more books."

In addition to wages, her employees required supervision and training. "We had a full-time employee and a part-time employee for a while, but I had a problem — was I managing people or writing new books?" Willie asks.

When she found herself without any employees at the beginning of 1999, Willie decided to take a break from being a boss. "We were putting all the money we made back into the company, and I was spending my time making sure everybody was doing what they should be doing. It was great to take a break and clean up the business."

Without employees, Willie was forced to learn how to use the computer. "Before I would give things to my employee and say, 'Type this up' or 'Check the e-mail for me.' Sometimes I'd ask her how she did something, and she'd show me, but I'd have no interest. I just did not want to do it.

"Now I've taken computer classes on QuickBooks, the Internet, QuarkXPress, Windows and Word. I've even played with a little design, laying out stuff. If I didn't have to get my next book to the distributor in four months, I could take the time to learn how to do some style pages. All my book formats are virtually the same. I'd love to know I could write a new book and import it right into a Quark layout, but there's no time to set that up."

Because Willie and her husband Mark did most of the work themselves without an employee in 1999, that was the year they earned their first decent profit. "In 1998 we made something like $1,500 after expenses. In 1999 our sales were $70,000 and our expenses were $40,000. So we made about $30,000."

Willie started Oakbrook Publishing House in 1996, and her first book, *Halloween School Parties...What Do I Do?*®, came out in 1996, followed by the first Valentine book, *Valentine School Parties...What Do I Do?*® in the summer of 1998 and the second Valentine book, *Valentine Boxes...What Do I Do?*®, in 2000. "In three years I've sold 12,000 copies of the Halloween book, around 9,000 copies of the Valentine's party book during its first two seasons, and shipped 2,000 copies of the Valentine box book for its first season."

Total sales for 2000 should be higher than for 1999 because of the new Christmas book, and sales in 2001 will be boosted by the slumber party book. "Once we get five books out, then we'll hire someone to market full time, or else an assistant to help us keep up with the daily publishing chores," Willie says. "I want to take a break from writing after the fifth book so I can clean up my piles, maybe cook a little."

Mark and Willie have discussed ways to free up more time, and concluded that they should pay somebody to do what they least like to do. "We determined that none of us likes cleaning, so we have someone cleaning our house now."

Getting Books Written

Willie's writing speed has increased substantially since she wrote her first book. "It's easier. I can sit down and completely write out a section. It can be done in five minutes if I've already tested the idea. And everything has to be tested; I won't put something in a book if it isn't."

She wrote her Valentine's box book during a family vacation. "We have a motor home and we drove it 20 hours each way to get there and back. The kids had their things to do, and I worked on my book. I had a little chart with hearts on it, a list of what I had to write. I just sat there and wrote. I'd tell Mark, 'Did another one! Did another one!' and I'd X in the little hearts.

"I'm way behind schedule on my Christmas book. Mark says if it comes down to it, we'll just get in the motor home during spring break so I can get it done. The doorbell won't ring, the dog won't be barking, people can't call me. I could whip it out."

Damaged Books

IPG has sent back to Willie over 200 damaged books. IPG charged a restocking fee as well as the shipping cost to send the books back to her. "Some look fine. Others the corners are bent a little, that type of thing, but at least I can sell them. I sell them for half price at special events I do , or if someone calls up and is real hesitant about paying $20, that's when we tell them we have damaged copies.

"I'll say, 'Well, they're slightly bent or I've written Do Not Remove on the covers for a show,' and they say, 'I don't care.' They jump on them for $10. So I have no problem taking damaged books back and selling them."

Willie sells 15% of her books directly, either to previous customers or to people calling her, and another 5% through her web site. Of the remaining books, 60% sell through bookstores, 5% through Quality Books to libraries, and the last 15% through toy or party stores, teacher stores, book shows or events.

Web Site

When the Halloween book first came out, Willie and Mark decided they needed to hire someone part-time. "One girl replied who was pretty young, a high school student. But she was very mature and she knew computers like crazy. She said, 'Oh, yeah, I've done my own web site.' I was going, 'You did your own web site!' She showed it to us, and I told Mark we had to hire her. She started for $5.00 per hour, and later we increased her pay to $7.00."

The web site pleased Willie. "It was and is very nice, although nothing fancy. But eventually I started to get 15-20 e-mails a week from people asking me how to order a book. I thought, 'It tells them how on the site. Why am I having to spend the time to individually e-mail order instructions to these people?'"

To find out why customers were getting confused, Willie took a hard look at her site. "I hadn't been in my own web site for a while. I thought, let's see, here's the ordering information button. I went into that page and everything was there. It said to call this number or send this or print this. So why were these people e-mailing me?"

She looked next at the information for one of her books. "I could see all the book information, and I'm imagining what people are doing. They click into the book to read about it, and they think, 'Oh, I really want this, how do I order it?' And there's no order button there. They have to go back to the home page to find the order button, but they don't do that. They e-mail me instead. So I had an order button put under the book information."

Willie thinks she's also improved her web site's effectiveness by slowing people down when they try to exit. "When they go to exit the site, they are asked, 'Exiting so soon? Did you check out how to win a free book?' It can click them back to a questionnaire for the next book in the series. If they fill it out and I use their interview, they get a free copy of that book. I think people are staying longer because suddenly I'm getting more e-mail responses."

Using her web site to collect information has been a real boon to Willie. "I always do interviews in the side columns of my books. Every single person I've interviewed in the last three years, I've used the interview. People think maybe their chances aren't that good, but I tell them we'll probably use it so they should fill out the questionnaire. They don't realize we're small and it's like, please, please, do it."

Willie agrees with the Rosses' suggestion to load people's names in a book. "They said that every single person you mention will want to buy your book. I give my interviewees a free copy, but for the Valentine's box book I sent out a letter with the free copy that said, 'Here's your free book and if you want a copy for Grandma or Grandpa, let us know and here's a discounted price.' I got people saying, 'Oh, I need one for Grandpa and one for Cousin, and can you sign it Dear Cousin So and So?' It really does help sell more books."

When the Kids Leave Home

All three of Willie's kids are now teenagers. "My oldest will be leaving for college in two years. In six years the last one will be eighteen. I'll have a lot more time to put into Oakbrook Publishing House, and the company can really take off."

In the meantime Willie limits her business growth in favor of taking care of her kids. "I still do things for my children's schools like chairing the Valentine's Day party for the middle school and working on the after-prom party for the high school. But I don't take on any long term projects like being the president of clubs."

Some of her activities will probably lead to additional book ideas for her series. "I've got to start doing more of the middle school and high school What Do I Do® books. And it's easy and fun to get ideas. For example, I was at the prom meeting and I was on top of the world. I'm not the kind of person who can sit for hours at a desk and work on the computer, but this was my forte. I love to create. I was saying, 'Ooh, we could do this, and this.' I was thrilled. Sometimes Mark asks me, 'Why are you doing this or that?' but I enjoy planning the parties and I learn so much." '

Though Willie struggles to find enough time to handle all her responsibilities, she enjoys her life. Although her main focus is her family, at the same time she's building something for the future. "I think the What Do I Do® series could become big," Willie says. "Oakbrook Publishing House could become a million dollar company. It's a matter of having the stamina and energy to get it there."

Chapter Three

The Hobby that Grew to Sell Over 100,000 Cookbooks Per Year

Virginia and Robert Hoffman started The Hoffman Press with the idea of having a hobby for their retirement years. "We moved to Santa Rosa about thirteen years ago when we retired. We were bored stiff and thought we could make $3,000 to $5,000 a year publishing a cookbook," Robert explains. Eight years after they printed their first book they are selling over 100,000 books per year.

Their original title was *The California Wine Country Cookbook*. "Virginia and I visited wineries and bought wine, and one day she noticed that the most recent cookbook offered for sale was over ten years old. She thought we ought to write our own book. I had worked in marketing and had done a lot of promotional stuff, so I said fine.

"In those days many wineries had executive chefs or catering firms so they could entertain the VIPs who visited, teach people how to buy and use wine, and host wine dinners for the public at a cost of up to $150 per person depending on the quality of the wines and the chef. Some of the chefs were world famous."

They collected 162 recipes from fifty-eight winery chefs in the Napa and Sonoma counties for *The California Wine Country*

Cookbook. "We tested the recipes before we included them in the book," Robert says. "Some of the best chefs had made mistakes, including some really funny ones. We checked all the recipes."

They decided on an initial print run of 5,000 because that gave them the best price break. "One day a big truck pulled up to our driveway and unloaded three large pallets of books. 'What have I done?' I thought as I looked at all of them."

Close to seventy years old at the time, Robert personally carried all the books into the garage because the truck driver couldn't help him. "Three weeks later the books were sold and Virginia and I were launched into publishing."

The Hoffmans were able to sell their first print run so quickly by partnering with the many wineries whose recipes were included in their book. "We had a little display stand for the books that the wineries could put in their gift shops. The top of the stand said 'We are in this cookbook' and gave the price, $12.95. Of course every winery in the book wanted copies."

The Hoffmans reprinted the book seven times before revising it in 1997. The revision was necessary because a lot of the chefs were no longer with the same wineries, and that caused some problems. "We didn't put the chefs' names in the second version," Robert says dryly. For the revised version they changed the title to *California Wine Country Cookbook II.*

Developing Cookbook Ideas

For their second book Virginia came up with the idea of doing a cookbook of turkey recipes, *The Great Turkey Cookbook.* "We felt turkey hadn't achieved the status as a staple that it should. So we spent months studying the market, statistics on sales, what people bought, how they prepared it, information like that." Their best source of information was Dr. Francine A. Bradley, the poultry specialist at the University of California at Davis.

"It took Virginia three years to gather all of the recipes. She created some and collected some from other sources," Robert says. Each recipe has a calorie count and nutritional information. The Hoffmans used software they bought from a supplier on the Internet to analyze their recipes.

Robert didn't think he had the marketing power to promote the turkey cookbook so he contacted the marketing manager at another publisher. "He asked us to come down and show it to him, and he bought it on the spot. The Crossing Press did a wonderful job for us; they got the turkey cookbook into the Book of the Month Club."

The Hoffmans decided to let The Crossing Press publish their next two books, *The Great Chicken Cookbook*, plus a small holiday cookbook called *The Holidays Cookbook*. The Crossing Press succeeded in selling book club rights for the holiday book to Book of the Month Club, and the chicken book to a German publisher. "BOMC used the holiday book as a premium if someone bought another book with them. We sold thousands of copies."

Though they enjoyed their relationship with The Crossing Press, they wanted to get back to publishing wine related books. "Their marketing of this type of book was not as qualified as was our own," Robert explains. "Subsequently we purchased the remaining inventory of our cookbooks that they had published and now market these books ourselves."

The Hoffmans currently have over ten different titles in print not including custom cookbooks. In 1999 they wrote and published *The Wine-Lover's Holidays Cookbook* as well as two custom cookbooks, one for a winery and another for an association of wineries. "Two new books are scheduled for the year 2000, plus two or three custom books as well," Robert says. Their best selling book so far is *Cooking with Wine*.

Sticking with Cookbooks

"Virginia comes up with the book concepts," Robert says. "We ask ourselves if there is a market for a book. Who would buy it and how many? If we agree that an idea is marketable then we go ahead and do it. We have had several opportunities to write books outside of the cookbook field, but we don't know how to market them. And we don't want to learn because we are doing so well at what we are doing."

Virginia has written or edited all of their books. Robert is emphatic that he is not looking for other authors to publish. "We don't want cookbook ideas; we are swamped with unbelievably bad stuff."

He advises would-be cookbook authors who are thinking about self-publishing to concentrate on niche cookbooks. "Unless she is famous, America doesn't care about your grandmother's recipes. They may be great recipes, but you won't sell books. There is a market for niche cookbooks. How about something for expectant mothers? Be specific."

By zeroing in on a particular market, Robert believes a small publisher's odds of success increase substantially. "We haven't had any marketing failures," Robert says. "We research how many books are out there, what their price range is, and that sort of thing. We study the market before we do a book. All of our books have made money. We won't print one if it won't."

The Publishing Side of Cookbooks

The Hoffmans spent two years researching the book business between the time they got the idea for their first book and when they had it printed. "We studied books. We had gone to at least five different seminars by the time we published our second book. We joined the Bay Area Publishers Association after our first book came out. We went to a meeting and that's how we learned about PMA."

Virginia spends a great deal of time and energy developing the right cover for their books. "The cover is for marketing. We don't have any repressed artistic desires that we feel we must express. We want a cover that will stand out. We design variations and then test them in the field. We put some dummy covers on a book and take them out on a weekend when there are lots of people in the stores to see how they do."

They put a book on the shelf and stand nearby waiting for people to pick it up. If no one does, they go home and start over with a new cover design. "But if they do reach for our test book, I thank them and tell them what it will be. I talk with them and get more good ideas than you ever dreamed of for book designs. In my opinion, an investment of a couple of hours doing this type of research can be the difference between the success and failure of a book. We get a strong cookbook cover each time."

Despite their reliance on testing to choose their covers, they don't let one opinion determine the fate of a cover. "Don't take the word of one gift store or bookstore owner. There are some great prejudices out there. We had a buyer who hated the cover of one of our books." The Hoffmans used the cover anyhow and sold more than 10,000 copies of that book in less than a year.

Taking the time to develop visually arresting covers has also paid off in getting additional publicity opportunities for The Hoffman Press cookbooks. "We received a phone call from a motion picture studio in Canada asking for permission to use one or more of our cookbooks in a forthcoming movie starring James Woods. The plot called for his wife to be an avid cook and consulting a cookbook in one or more scenes."

The studio discovered the books by surfing the Internet. "They thought the covers were interesting. They were very business-like. They faxed us a request for permission along with a synopsis of the movie, and a list of the three books they wished to use."

The cost to create each cover varies widely. "Virginia was an interior designer so she designs the cover layouts. They are executed by various artists." Extra book covers are used as mailers to reviewers, potential buyers, and in promotional materials. Some cover fronts are cut to postcard size and used that way.

Unlike many cookbook publishers, the Hoffmans don't use photos of the food. "We have published seventeen cookbooks without photos because the photos must be in color. Color photos would take our books out of the price range that we like."

Alternative Places to Sell Books

A large part of the Hoffmans' success in selling cookbooks has been where they sell them. "Retail book stores are not a good place to sell books; they are terrible," Robert states unequivocally. "If you can't find a place to sell books outside of bookstores, then you shouldn't do it....unless you are rich and famous."

Instead, the Hoffmans hired reps to get their books nationwide into gift stores and winery tasting rooms, wine shops and liquor shops. Robert found his first reps by faxing five medium size wine tasting rooms back East. He asked for the names of the three best reps who called on them. "I told them that if they were good enough to do this for me, I would send them one of our books. We got three responses and that's how we got our first reps."

Robert has repeated this process over the years, either faxing retailers or visiting them on field trips to ask for the names of the best reps with whom they do business. "Some reps have been good and some bad, awful in fact, but we are very happy with the ones we have now."

The reps are paid 15% or 20% of the wholesale price of the books, depending on whether they are master reps or a rep organization. The Hoffmans currently have twelve reps for their books in the gift and liquor fields, and 80% of their sales are made outside of bookstores. "We have recently widened our distribution in the gift market field with the appointment of several new sales representatives and by securing several wholesalers in the gift market."

Robert offers incentives with the seasons to help generate orders. "We have different promotions. In the spring we offer 90 day terms and in the fall we give the stores free freight. We keep the marketing people apprised of what we are doing, for example giving a special pre-publication price for the gift market.

"Our main thrust of marketing will continue to be the national gift market field. We have increased our presence on the Internet substantially by getting our books placed on many wine related web sites. Direct mail will be increased this coming year because we found it to be highly effective this past fall."

Hiring Help

Robert makes it clear that someone doesn't have to be technologically savvy to be a publisher. "You don't have to be a computer geek to be in business. Hire someone to help you. One thing that deters people is they say they can't run a computer. I didn't have a computer until four years ago."

The Hoffmans originally hired a secretary who worked part-time out of her home to typeset their first books. When they eventually parted ways, the Hoffmans found somebody else through a publishers' chat group. Now that they have a computer, they've hired a technician to come once a month to clear up any problems in their files and hard drive. "We found him through the Internet and he is a nice guy; we're very pleased. We had someone else design the web site for us."

Reporters who visit the site find out about their books and contact the Hoffmans to obtain review copies. "We are delighted to send them, but only if the reporters are reputable. We check them out. We used to send review copies to anyone who asked, but we aren't so lovable anymore."

Originally their site, www.foodandwinecookbooks.com, was located with other web sites for books, but the Hoffmans weren't selling their cookbooks. "We went to seminars in the food industry about online marketing, and realized that people don't go to book sites looking for cookbooks; they look at food and wine sites. So we moved our site to a wine location, and now our books sell. We learned that if you want to have a successful web site, identify with the topic, not with the fact that you are selling books. Our books are kitchen accessories."

Though Robert believes that many online buyers leave his site to buy his books at more well known Internet bookstores such as Amazon.com, he values the direct sales he gets. "If you pass sales along to an online bookstore instead of fulfilling them yourself, you are giving away the single best advantage of selling directly, a mailing list of people who are real prospects for your books. We also get wholesale inquiries. Some have amounted to orders of thirty-six books at a time and have become repeat accounts. In addition, when we do a new book, we can offer it at a prepublication discount to these people and get a surprising number of sales."

Sales through Amazon.com have been modest, but consistent. "Several of our books were offered by Amazon.com before we applied to their Advantage program. We sent in all the info as requested and in about ten days we were in the program. The sales of the eight books we have from them increased by about 500%. We get one or two orders from them for books every week." Though joining the Advantage program meant giving a larger discount, Robert believes the additional sales are worth it.

As a method for selling books, book signings aren't at the top of his list of marketing activities. "They are a lot of fun, but not productive. If your time is valuable, you won't sell enough books to make it worthwhile."

The Hoffmans use Ingram, Baker & Taylor, and several regional wholesalers to handle bookstore sales. Unlike gift stores, the bookstores can return unsold books. "We don't like returns any more than any publisher does, but if you don't have some books returned, then the stores aren't carrying enough of your books."

Remaindered Books

When the Hoffmans come out with a new edition of a cookbook, they sell the leftovers of the previous edition as remainders. "The going rate seems to be about 10% or less. The tops we have received for a $14.95 retail priced cookbook is $1.50. The buyer pays the freight and they usually want at least a couple hundred copies."

Robert finds his buyers on the Internet. "There are many places that will buy remainders. Put remainder books in your favorite search engine. Send each place a description of what you have and offer to send a sample copy."

Revising books has paid off for The Hoffman Press. "One of our books sold about 5,000 copies its first year, but four years later it was down to about 1,500 copies per year. We did a revised edition and sales went back up to 5,000."

Printing and Shipping Books

For short print runs of custom cookbooks, the Hoffmans use KNI in Los Angeles. Otherwise, they always print 5,000 or more copies of their books and use Bertelsmann Industry Services, also in Los Angeles. "When they say a book will be ready in three weeks, it's usually ready in two. Their quality is superlative."

Rayve Fulfillment of Windsor, California, ships out orders for them. "We have used and recommended Rayve for years. We

were their first account, and they have a new and larger warehouse now in Santa Rosa with a full time manager. They are very
good and handle everything for us. Whether a publisher has one
book or twenty doesn't make any difference to them.

"People can fax their orders to us. We have a dedicated fax
machine. Or they can call Rayve's 1-800 number that appears in
the back of each of our books and on our web site. Rayve stores
our books and picks and packs our shipments ranging in size
from one book to a pallet load. Their fees are fair and the service
is impeccable. We could not operate without them."

Productive and Enjoyable Work

The Hoffmans believe in contracting out as much of the work
as possible. Robert and Virginia focus on what they do best: marketing and writing new cookbooks. They hire people to handle
everything else. "Virginia creates and write the recipes, handles
the designs of the books, and oversees the finances of the firm. I
handle production and marketing.

"We work a four or five day week. I am at the computer
from 7:00 till 9:00 in the morning, marketing on the Internet and
phone from 9:00 to 12:00, lunch from 12:00 to 2:00, and work
till 4:00. Virginia follows the same schedule except that she starts
at 10:00. We used to work six and seven days each week, but
soon learned that we get more done this way. We spend eight to
ten weeks a year in the field visiting various wine producing re-
gions in the United States, Canada and Europe."

When deciding what work to do themselves and what to
contract out, the Hoffmans value their time at $150 per hour. "If
we can get the work done for less by someone else, we do. If it
costs more than that, and we can do it ourselves, we do. Our
typesetting and proofreading, fulfillment services and web sites
are done by others."

The Hoffmans run their press with an eye on the bottom line, but they also enjoy a high level of personal satisfaction in their work. "You write a cookbook for one of four reasons," Robert says bluntly. "You really want to impart knowledge, you want to be with other publishers so you can belong somewhere, you want to keep busy, or you want to make money. The Hoffman Press is in business to make money.

"But most importantly, Virginia and I are still enjoying ourselves. Creativity, regardless of the form it takes, is stimulating. Our creation of new books, the new markets for them, and the knowledge that we are creating culinary pleasure for the public that buys our books is more rewarding than anything else we have ever done."

Chapter Four

Published Author Takes Control

Many people assume that the only reason writers self-publish is because they can't get published any other way. Peter Kent, however, previously sold the rights for approximately forty computer books to other publishers before he began his own company, Top Floor Publishing. "I wanted more control over the process," Peter explains. "I've written good books, books that I was told were good, yet they did very badly thanks to screw-ups on the part of the publishers."

Mistakes ranged from not listing a book in Bowker's *Books in Print* to promised promotional campaigns that never materialized. "In one case they decided not to promote the series my book was in for one season because something else came up that they wanted to promote instead." That season, unfortunately, was when Peter's book was published.

Issues of quality also bothered him. "One of the problems for computer books in particular is that everything moves too fast, and most big computer book companies have relatively low production standards. I've had a lot of embarrassing mistakes in my books such as pictures in the wrong places, captions that don't match the pictures, or jokes printed without their punch lines."

Therefore Peter was particularly pleased by the comment of one reviewer on his first self-published title, *Poor Richard's Web*

Site. "He told me it was the only book he ever reviewed that didn't have mistakes in it. I didn't bother to tell him that there were mistakes that he'd missed. It wasn't a perfect book, but it was a lot better than any of the books I'd done before for other publishers."

Getting a Distributor

Peter believes the general public didn't recognize his name when he first published *Poor Richard's Web Site*. Having a track record in the publishing world, however, did help him get IPG to carry his book. "I knew the woman who ordered computer books for Borders. She actually told this distributor to take me because she wanted to buy my book. That was very handy because it's difficult for a small publisher to get a good distributor."

IPG has continued to handle all of Top Floor's sales to book wholesalers and bookstores. "They give discounts to the wholesalers and bookstores, and then they take their share of the net receipts. For instance, for every retail dollar, a wholesaler like Ingram takes $.55 and IPG takes its share of the remaining $.45, and I get what's left."

Despite receiving a fraction of his retail prices, Peter is content. "There's no way I'm going to handle bookstore distribution. It would be an absolute nightmare. I dread to think of the amount of time and effort it would take me to ship so many books, do all the billing, and handle the collections."

Peter thinks Jason Olim, one of his co-authors for the second book he published, *The CDnow Story*, has the right idea. "He says you've got to look at the supply chain and figure out what you can do best in that chain. Distributing books to bookstores is not something a small publisher can do best, quite frankly. A small publisher should focus on what he can do best: create good books. That's what I'm trying to do."

Because IPG picked up Peter's first book after it was already in print, the title didn't make it into their catalog as a new book. "They did a flyer to tell their sales reps about it, but how many of the flyers really got to the reps?" Peter wonders. "I didn't entirely miss that season, but *Poor Richard's Web Site* undoubtedly didn't do as well as it could have. And when the next catalog came around it was backlisted because by then it was old."

Despite this problem, Peter's first print run of 5,000 books lasted him only six months. For his second printing he ordered an additional 5,300 copies. His third print run brought the total copies in print of the first edition to approximately 16,000. "I sent off about 1,000 review copies," Peter says. "I think *Poor Richard's Web Site* has been the most reviewed computer book ever."

It took some time for Peter to get his first book into Barnes & Noble. His reputation inside the book business eventually helped him to get a sizeable first order for 700 copies. "They knew I was a best selling computer book author, so the name helped me to some degree to get into their stores. They knew I had a track record and that my book would be of a decent quality."

Radio Shows, Book Signings, and Seminars

"I did loads of radio shows at the start," Peter says, "maybe 50 or 60. I didn't see a huge number of sales. Some people do very well on the radio and they can sell 10, 20, or 30 copies each show. My first book didn't sell that way. It was expensive and not the typical radio show book, not a book about how to make money from antiques in your attic or how to get a job without writing a resume. I only saw radio sales dribbling in here and there."

Book signings aren't high on Peter's list of the best ways to promote his books, either. "I think they are a really great way to waste a lot of time unless you've got a way to work them. Some people hit all the local media and do interviews and give several book signings in a day, and if you can put that together then maybe it's worthwhile. But generally for book signings, you go in, sit around for awhile, and sell three books. After the bookstore and distributor take their share, you make just a few bucks per book.

"You might end up spending several hours when you include your travel time and getting there a little early to chat with the staff. It's better to do seminars or lectures. I think speeches and lectures are a great way to sell books because you sell the book directly and you don't have to split the sales price with anyone."

Promoting Books Online

Peter has had the most success with online promotion. "If you ignore Internet marketing, you are cutting off your nose to spite your face," Peter states. "It is so powerful and cheap, it would be crazy not to use it. Internet marketing built my company."

Peter highly recommends e-mailing journalists online. "It works well if you can get a list of e-mail addresses for journalists, and you can buy these lists. I don't regard this as spam because these people have requested to be on a PR list. You can get a fantastic response.

"If you use the right software and maybe do an e-mail merge, you can send out a couple of thousand of these e-mails to journalists. But I only send them to people who I think are appropriate. For instance, I e-mailed music and computer journalists for my MP3 book. Within ten minutes you can get journalists saying that they'll take a look at a review copy. It's great.

"My whole Poor Richard's series has been built by Internet marketing on a shoestring budget. My first book, *Poor Richard's Web Site*, hit the best seller list at Amazon.com for a short while and became the most widely reviewed and praised title in computer book history. It was all based on Internet marketing."

Peter is astonished at how few of the big companies understand how to do business on the Internet. "They use the old business world model. They spend huge bucks on paid advertising like banner ads. But the Internet provides an incredible way to connect with people at a very low cost.

"You should make sure you're registered everywhere you can be, let newsletter editors know about your products, offer giveaways and review copies to related web sites, and build a list of journalists, web sites, and newsletters that are interested in your products and keep them up to date with special offers. This stuff takes time, but very little money."

Adding Titles

Peter co-wrote his second title, *The CDnow Story*, with Jason Olim and Matthew Olim, the twin co-founders of CDnow. He released it about a year after publishing *Poor Richard's Web Site*. "IPG considered it one of their top new titles. I got four pages in both the business and computer catalogs. They told me it was getting really good advance orders. In fact, I received a call from somebody at IPG telling me he thought the book would go nuts once it got into the bookstores." Overall sales, though, were fewer than Peter had hoped for.

He followed up within the next year with two more Poor Richard titles. *Poor Richard's Internet Marketing and Promotions* was co-written with Tara Calishain, and *Poor Richard's E-mail Publishing* was written by Chris Pirillo. Peter also published a stand-alone title, *MP3 and the Digital Music Revolution*, by John Hedtke.

Looking back at his first five books, Peter thinks it would have been better if he had focused his energy on the books in his Poor Richard series. "Those books really chugged along. When I looked at the rankings on Amazon.com, *E-mail Publishing* would be under 5,000 and *Internet Marketing and Promotions* even lower. *Poor Richard's Web Site*'s ranking wasn't so good before the new edition came out, but then it bounced back up. *The CDnow Story* ranking wasn't bad, but not as good as the series books. And the MP3 book didn't do terribly well."

The results brought home to him the power of developing a series. "Bookstore buyers understand series. They think, 'Okay, *Poor Richard's Web Site* did well, so we'll buy *Poor Richard's Internet Marketing and Promotions* and *Poor Richard's E-mail Publishing*.' Publishing books in a series makes each subsequent book much easier to market," Peter explains.

During his third year Peter published two more stand-alone books, *The Official Miva Web-Scripting Book* and *MP3 for Musicians*, plus two special editions. "For one of the special editions, we took chapters from three Poor Richard books for MacMillan Digital Publishing to bundle with a software CD produced by my other business, BizBlast.com. I was willing to do this because I regarded it as a sales piece and didn't think it would harm sales for the original books. We called it *Poor Richard's Guide to Electronic Commerce: Geek-Free Commonsense Advice for Doing Business on the Internet*. The second special edition was a small version of the e-mail publishing book, about half the size, which we sold to an e-mail publishing company to give away as a premium."

Hiring Someone to Run Top Floor

About a year after starting Top Floor, Peter founded another business, an Internet service company called BizBlast.com, to help small businesses work online. "It was an opportunity I couldn't refuse, but it was tough. I was working 16 hour days and going crazy. I had promised books that were already in the catalog, written and paid for, so I had to deliver them."

Printing the new books required capital, and Peter had to scramble for funds. "I was running in the red. I covered the bills using credit cards because I didn't get a salary from Bizblast.com for over a year."

Busy with the new company, Peter knew he needed someone to help him keep Top Floor going. Finding the right person wasn't easy, but he found success through a bit of luck. "While at a sales meeting in New York, I had a beer and a chat with the president of IPG, Kurt Matthews. I told him I had to hire somebody because of this other business, but I was having problems. He told me I should hire Missy Derkacz. She used to work for IPG in Chicago, but had moved to Denver."

Because he didn't have the cash flow for a large salary, Peter offered Missy a part of the company. "Understand that I couldn't just hire an assistant; I had to hire someone who was capable of running Top Floor and who would do a good job without being watched. She took a pay cut when she first joined Top Floor, but I gave her equity in the company that vests over a few years."

Within months Peter was able to raise Missy's salary to its previous level as his publishing company started to produce cash flow again. "We went from two books to seven in a little more than a year. Though we would sell the company if we got the right offer, all I'm interested in for now is to see Top Floor self-sustaining and growing at a reasonable rate for the next two to three years. By then Bizblast.com may have been bought, and I'll be out. If so, I'll still have a publishing company to play with."

Missy worked for a while out of Peter's house, and then from her home, but they soon started to look for an office space as well as for an assistant for Missy. "We hired someone to do the book layout. We had been using contract people, but it was a hassle. Sometimes they exaggerated their hours and overcharged us. Other times they couldn't turn the work around quickly enough. We believed we could bring our cost of producing our books down quite a bit by bringing it in-house."

The economics started to make sense because of the number of books they planned to do. "If we do six or eight books this year we can almost pay for the salary just on the savings on layout costs."

Selling Over the Internet

In addition to selling his Top Floor books through his web site, Peter also sells books he has written for other publishers. Customers can fill in a form at the web site, or they can print it out and either fax it or mail it to Top Floor. "I used to have Bookmasters handle phone orders, but we decided to stop doing that. The number of phone orders used to be much higher, but it really went down. I guess people don't worry about security ordering online any more."

If people don't want to buy directly from him, Peter lets them buy from Amazon.com through his site. "It's easier for them to buy from Amazon because customers can get one click ordering. If they've bought from Amazon before, they may want to do it again because it's just less hassle. Click, bang, it's ordered. I get paid through the Amazon affiliate program."

Peter maintains contact with thousands of potential customers through his e-newsletter about web sites called *Poor Richard's Web Site News*. It goes out every month to over 50,000 people in more than 100 countries.

Sales through Amazon.com, however, far exceed the number of sales through his own web site. Peter keeps an eye on the reviews that get posted about his titles to make sure that they are legitimate. "Amazon will take down reviews if they have a good reason. One review was obviously an ad for a web site. They were posting reviews for books on Amazon saying, 'This is okay, but it doesn't have as much information as such and such web site.'

"This review appeared for my technical writing book, so I went to the recommended web site. There was no information about technical writing on the site. I contacted Amazon, they agreed it was an ad, and they took the review down."

Sometimes reviews are bad, but legitimate. "Then I'll get people who like that book to post positive reviews. That turns it around. The reviews are important for any type of book. Authors should check to see what their reviews are on Amazon."

Finding and Selecting Authors

In order to grow his company more quickly and to take advantage of other people's expertise, Peter looked for co-authors early on, and then for people to write complete books. "I push my authors a bit," Peter says. "I want good writing and content. I'll ask an author, 'Why are you writing this, and why aren't you telling the reader that?' I want to make sure readers get the information they need."

Peter finds his authors through a variety of ways. "I use the network," Peter says. "I had gone to my old agent and said we were looking for an author for a Poor Richard's book on online communities. He said some friends of mine, Margie and John Levine, a brother and sister team, wanted to do a book on that very subject. The Levines, the authors of *The Internet for Dummies*, had been shopping their new idea around, but the big computer book companies weren't interested because their book idea wasn't focused tightly enough on technology. It wasn't about building online communities using a particular software or technology. The Levines knew what I was doing with Top Floor and they respected my work, so they signed a contract with me."

When Peter and Missy decided to do a Poor Richard book on affiliate marketing, Missy spent time visiting affliate-related web sites. "That's one way to find writers these days. Find out who's writing about a particular subject already, and the lovely thing is you can actually see what their writing is like," Peter says with satisfaction. "If someone has a web site and they're writing newsletters, you can see their articles at their site before ever asking them for a proposal."

A few book ideas have been sent to Top Floor unsolicited. "I get people e-mailing me asking if I'm interested in such and such a book. Once or twice I've said yes, but I never heard from them again. All of the books we've done have been our ideas. That's pretty typical of the computer book business."

Peter's qualifications for an author have changed a bit as he's gained more experience as a publisher. "We've been looking just at an author's ability to write, but now we're doing more work on getting authors who do promotion. The Levines have a huge e-mail list because in the e-mail chapter of their book *The Internet for Dummies* they encouraged people to contact them.

"Chris Perillo, who wrote *Poor Richard's E-mail Publishing*, is good to work with because he's got an e-newsletter that goes out to 160,000 people. His book was on an Amazon.com bestseller list before it was even in print. It went from a ranking of 640,000 to 43 after Chris mentioned the book in his newsletter. Plus Chris hired a public relations firm to promote his newsletter. Obviously that's going to help the book as well. In fact, we sent a bunch of review books to the PR company."

Peter believes in being generous with more than review copies. He thinks publishers should encourage their authors to sell books by giving them sizeable discounts. "This always used to irritate me as an author. I'd write the book and then they would say, 'If you need more books, we would be happy to sell them to you at 40% off.' I'm not stupid. I know they're selling the books to other people at a lower rate. If they could make money selling to Ingram at a 55% discount, why couldn't they give me a 55% discount?"

Peter thinks publishers should do as much as they can for their authors. "You want your author on your side. I would love to have my authors buying 1,000 copies at our 60% author discount and selling them at seminars. I would still make enough money on the book, and the book would be getting promoted.

"I try to pay my authors decent advances. We're paying somewhere between $5,000-$9,000." Peter thinks these advance amounts are competitive with the other major computer book publishers.

Problems with Authors

Top Floor has experienced a few problems with its authors. "A couple of books are late. One is months and months late. It's very irritating," Peter says. He finds it difficult to plan a publishing schedule or promote a book early when he doesn't know when, or if, a manuscript is actually going to show up.

Occasionally a manuscript flunks the quality test. "Missy will look at the manuscript and if she thinks there's a problem, she'll ask me what I think. On one book we ended up with a bunch of chapters that I would not use. I would have killed the book before I put those chapters in it. It had to be cleaned up, and of course that delayed the book considerably."

Sometimes even after an author has signed a contract to write a book, the deal falls through, leaving Missy and Peter searching for a replacement author. "We found two people who were willing to do the affiliate book, but no one actually started on it. I still think we'll end up getting a good book, but I'm not quite sure," Peter says.

Earning Extra Money

"If you step back and look at the publishing business for a moment, you can see a number of areas that are potentially very lucrative," Peter says. "There are things you can do to leverage the work you've already done to bring in additional money with relatively little effort. One of these areas is foreign rights. You've already created a book, so why not make more money with a little extra work? We hand over the electronic files to a foreign publisher for a couple of thousand dollars, and later on they give us more money as the books sell."

Though *Poor Richard's Web Site* has already been translated into German, and an Italian publisher agreed to take several of the Poor Richard books, Peter plans to pay more attention to the potential for foreign rights sales. "The Germans gave us a $2,500 advance and then every six months we get a check for several thousand more. Selling foreign rights is great; it's like money for nothing because the book is already done. But it can be quite difficult to get the foreign rights sales, and we need to find an agent to do this for us."

Peter would also like to put together more special sales. "If somebody wants a special edition, it is really easy to turn it around. It's not a lot of work. You've only got somebody's time to layout the new edition, and then, bang, you have a new book that could bring in tens of thousands of dollars."

What He Would Have Done Differently

"I wish I would have done a bit more to brighten up the covers for the series books right from the start," Peter says. His original covers were beautifully done, but too subtle. "They were not clear enough in the bookstores. I needed something where the title of the book really popped out at a distance. The question to ask is, 'If I hold up this book across the room, does the title stand out?' The new style is really chunky and the title is quite clear. It's brighter and, I think, more attractive."

Though Top Floor has published several books that were not in the Poor Richard series, Peter intends to steer away from those types of books in the future. "Most books are going to go in the series because they're easier to sell. People recognize the name."

Top Floor's Mission

"In the field of computer books, a lot of the titles out there don't provide real information," Peter says. "Many are rehashes of user manuals. A lot of the time I think, where's the meat? A significant number are just bad. I think some of the big computer book companies don't understand how to create good books.

"I believe a good book is one where the readers come away knowing a lot more than when they started to read it. I'm interested in the writing and the content. I want to make sure my readers have real information."

As well as focusing on quality content, Peter wants to publish a different type of computer book. "Most of the computer books focus very tightly on some sort of technology. They are what I call 'point and click books.' I don't want books on various software products; I want books on how to get something done using computers, whether that's building a web site or doing Internet marketing. That's where I'm trying to push the Poor Richard series."

Looking back at his decision to start Top Floor Publishing, Peter has no regrets. "Publishing is not an easy way to make a living. But if a book and its promotion aren't done right, I've got only myself to blame."

Overall Peter believes he has done a better job with his books compared to what would have happened if they had been published by someone else. "The idea that if you write a good book, it will turn into a best seller is nonsense. Your book may be good, but if the publisher does a bad job, it won't matter. I've got more control over my books now, and that makes them better."

Chapter Five

Making a Living with One Book

Rare indeed is the self-publisher who can make a living by publishing only one book. Yet Barbara Hudgins' first title, *New Jersey Day Trips*, has supported her for over a decade. She has sold more than 95,000 copies and is currently working on the ninth edition. "People say you have to have one book, then two books, and then four books, but you don't have to be big in that way," she explains.

Barbara landed in the field of travel writing by accident. Back in 1978 her husband wanted her to make some extra money, but he didn't want her to work full-time. Barbara got a job working part-time at a little advertising agency. "The agency had only one client, a real estate company. I wrote real estate ads and brochures for them. Then the client decided they wanted the sort of booklet a lot of real estate agencies put out, something that profiled the town and the area."

Barbara went to the library to look up information for the booklet. "I found two or three books that were pretty bad. The one major book was practically just a listing of the places without any editorializing, no judgement, no reviewing. I remember throwing it across the room. And that's where the germ of the idea of doing a New Jersey book came from. I realized that New Jersey was dominated in the south by Philadelphia and in the north by New York. The local library, for example, had about ten books on New York."

Using the one book that was any good at all, Barbara started to go to places. Since she was a young mother, she took her two pre-teen children with her and came up with another way to make some money. "I began to write articles for a local newspaper about going on day trips. I called it "Trips & Treks". My husband didn't make that much money so it was a convenience to write for a newspaper about trips. It meant I could get into places for free.

"I used to go to museums and parks with my kids, so we were doing these sorts of things anyway. And we usually took a week or two down at the Jersey shore and went to places there, as well."

For two years Barbara continued to write ads and a few brochures for the real estate company, working about ten hours per week, and sold her articles to the newspaper for $15 each. "As I wrote the articles, I kept them. And then a friend said that she kept a scrapbook of all my articles so she could refer to them when she went on trips. I thought, 'Gee, if somebody takes the trouble to put my articles in a scrapbook, I might as well do it for them.' Obviously the time had come for me to put a book together."

The First Few Editions

Barbara's first edition was plagued by problems. "A friend of mine did most of the book design. She had worked as the designer for the booklets I wrote for the advertising agency. She had started her own company and she did the book with me on a sort of consignment basis. She did the illustrations and design, and marked it up for the printer. We used the same printer who did her brochures.

"He wasn't a book printer, and that was my first mistake. And she didn't know anything about the book business, and neither did I, so we did everything wrong. We didn't know anything about ISBN numbers, or that if you just put a paper cover on a book it will smudge. Nobody told us about laminating covers. We didn't even go for a real cover paper. We used the type of paper that was used on programs at the local theaters, maybe a little heavier than that."

The second mistake was getting the job misquoted. "The designer asked the printer how much it would cost to print 2,000 copies. I think it was something like $1.00 per copy, which sounded reasonable to me. But she forgot to ask him how much it would cost to typeset the book first, so I ended up getting a bill for $3,000 instead of $2,000."

Fortunately for Barbara, her friend took the responsibility for the $1,000 error because it had been her job to handle getting the book printed. "She said she wouldn't take anything until I made my money back. I broke even on that one, so neither of us made any money. She didn't care because she wanted a book, something she could say she had designed. I was very lucky that we didn't have a falling out."

It took Barbara two years to sell the first edition. "I went around to the local bookstores, and that's when people told me the cover wasn't good enough. It's so different for me now. If I print up 6,000 copies, I know I can sell them fairly easily."

For Barbara's second edition, she went to a graphic arts house. "They had only done one book, but at least the woman there was much more knowledgeable about basic design. She had experience with magazines."

Barbara didn't discover Dan Poynter's book until her third edition. "New publishers have a lot more information available to them today than I did. By the time I read Dan's book, I had made most of the mistakes."

Changing the Name of Her Book

Barbara's title for her first edition was the same as her newspaper column. "I thought *Trips & Treks* was a cute name, but it was another mistake," she says. "When you do a travel or regional book, you should say what it is. By changing the name to *New Jersey Day Trips*, booksellers could find it listed with Baker & Taylor, and customers could find it in the bookstores. If a person looked for books about New Jersey, there it was, alphabetically under the Ns."

Over the years, Barbara has noticed a change in the way her competitors' books are titled. "Amazon.com has changed everything. They list numbers before letters. If you check a category in Amazon.com, say New Jersey guidebooks, you'll get the 10 Best Hikes, the 15 Best Bike Rides, the 100 Best This or That. People have figured it out, and they don't write out the number, they use the number itself."

Barbara has stuck with her book's second name because of the recognition she has built up over the years, but she has expanded her geographic territory to include some sites in New York and Pennsylvania.

Getting Divorced and Serious about Sales

Barbara and her husband divorced in 1988. "My son was still in high school, and by that time I was selling around 5,000 or 6,000 copies a year. For my first edition I had a very low price: $6.95. Then I raised it to $7.95, but because the distributors took 55%, I wasn't making very much money, about $5,000-$6,000 per year. I had to make more money. I had to start raising the price."

Today the price has reached $12.95, and Barbara averages over 6,000 copies sold per year. "For the past nine years I've netted somewhere between $23,000 and $36,000 each year. That's how much I take in from bookstores, wholesalers and direct sales minus the cost of the physical books, meaning typesetting, pictures, cover, printing, and freight to me from the printer."

Barbara's sales vary with the age of the edition of her book. "The first year a new edition is out I might net $45,000, and the second year $22,000. I do make a little extra from related things like slide talks, my newspaper column, and occasional articles. That usually adds a bit less than $1,000 per year."

During her best year, 1996, Barbara had gross profits that exceeded $50,000, but on average they are half of that. "I don't know how to sell more than 10,000 copies in one year. That's about the most I've sold. There are so many competing books. I have to share the market, and there are only so many people who are going to buy a book on New Jersey."

One practice that allows Barbara to live well on a modest income is her ability to deduct expenses from her income. "I'll go down to the Jersey shore and take off whatever the guy who does my taxes says I can. I also belong to a theater group that goes five times a year to New York to see the shows, and I take off the bus trip and the lunch.

"Because of the nature of my book, my research for it is mixed with social days out. I go on a lot of bus trips. Once in a while I'll be sitting next to somebody and she'll say, 'I took the day off work because I wanted to see this place so much.' And I'll be going there as part of my job.

"Or else I'll go down to Atlantic City with my daughter. People will ask me how much I gambled at the tables, but I go down there to look at the sites. I have to go to keep my book current and so I can be up-to-date when I give talks. Things keep changing all the time. My book is 75% research and 25% writing."

Barbara's best sales months are April through July when people buy the book for themselves, and then again in December when they purchase it as a gift. "In August sales start to taper off,

September through October are slow, but Christmas is always a good season," Barbara says. "January is the worst."

The Costs of Printing

"My first printing of a new edition costs around $2.50 per book, and the second printing is $1.35 or so. The first printing includes a lot of one-time expenses like the typesetting. That always costs me $3,000. I can't put it to disk on my own computer because of problems my machine has with other machines. Maybe that will change someday, but for now I still make hand corrections and pay someone to do the typesetting."

Instead of using a local typesetter for her eighth edition, Barbara tried to save money by having her printer do the typesetting for her. "I hated it. It wasn't Gilliland's fault; you just can't have typesetting done by osmosis or telephone." Barbara will bring the typesetting closer to home for the next edition so she can easily double-check the work.

Pictures are readily available and affordable for Barbara to include in her book. "Pictures are easy to get. I'll call up the local Chamber of Commerce or the particular museum or amusement park, and they'll send me pictures. I'll change some pictures from one edition to the next to freshen it up a bit. Then of course I have to put in new captions."

Reviews, Book Signings and Talks

Barbara prefers to have an article written about her rather than receive a review of her book. "I did get a lot of reviews, but many reviewers feel they have to be critical. Luckily, this was a book that almost everybody liked. But articles are better than reviews to get bookstores interested in you."

A distributor first showed interest in Barbara's book after an article appeared. "They called me about carrying my book. But straight reporting articles can be a problem. They don't give you something to quote like a review does."

Barbara has handled this problem by writing her own best blurb and putting it in bold letters on the back of her book. The quote appears without any attribution, but carries the weight of an endorsement. "It says, 'The most helpful guidebook ever written about New Jersey,' and then I list what the newest edition includes that wasn't in the last version."

Because her book has been around for years, Barbara doesn't try to get reviews anymore. "I've gotten lazy because the book has legs now." She still does book signings and speaks to local groups. "When I do talks for groups like the Newcomers Club I'll do a slide show. I have an old Kodak carousel. It holds 80 slides so I give 30 seconds to each slide. Of course, the book always sells well after something like that. If it's a luncheon for 40 people, I usually sell 10-15 copies."

In order to encourage this type of direct sale, Barbara offers a discount. "I find it much easier to sell the book for $10. It gives them an incentive to buy and since I include the sales tax, I don't have to make change, except maybe for a $20 bill."

As a plus, each time she speaks to a group, her appearance is written up in the group's newsletter. "People sometimes think publicity is only getting attention from the big media, but this kind of thing is good for a regional book."

Barbara also teaches classes on self-publishing through a local adult education program. "They don't pay me very much, but I do it for the exposure. I limit the class to 20 people, but the class brochure is sent to 50,000 people. And partly I do it because people ask me about my business. Rather than go through it again and again, I tell them I'm giving a class."

Definition of Success

"When I went to college, the theory was that if you were supposed to be a great writer, you would work at a warehouse or something stupid like that during the day, and then go home and write the Great American Novel at night. But it just doesn't work out that way," Barbara says.

"I think the explosion of self-publishing has given many people a chance to do what they want to do and not be dependent on some editor at some publishing house to make a decision as to whether their work is worthy or not. I belong to a writers' group, and they feel that if they can make their work better, it will be accepted. But that isn't always true. Sometimes the editor rejects a manuscript because he has just spent his entire budget on some celebrity biography.

"The idea of being able to do what you want to do and make a living at it is very important," Barbara emphasizes. "That's success. Years ago I did have a few articles in magazines, but it was very frustrating. When you work for somebody else, you do it their way. However, I'm completely free to set up my book exactly the way I want to do it. Initially I wasn't so in love with going to places in New Jersey, but travel writing, as it turns out, is very pleasant."

Chapter Six

350,000 Books Sold by Making Premium Sales

Diane Pfeifer wrote and published country music songs for years before she got the idea to do a popcorn cookbook. "I believed the world needed a popcorn cookbook. I love popcorn, and I thought surely there must be a lot of other people who get excited about it, too."

She decided to publish her book by herself. "I thought it was the same sort of business as writing and selling songs. I knew how to get songs to certain producers and get the songs promoted on radio. But I didn't realize that when you are a book publisher, you are basically a manufacturer. You have to have money to make money. When I was in the music business, the most I invested was about $100 in recording the demo of a song. I had all these friends who were musicians, and we did each other's songs for free."

Printing her first book, however, required a substantial amount of cash, especially since Diane decided to do a large print run. "All of a sudden, I had 10,000 books in my garage. Still, I thought it was going to be a drop in the bucket for what I would need. I started taking *For Popcorn Lovers Only* around to the local gift shops. In the beginning I put my books on consignment, and of course it was a nightmare, but eventually they sold. It taught me a lot about marketing."

Within two months, Diane received a large premium order. "I had approached TV Time Popcorn. I walked into this guy's office, and he offered me $20,000 for 5,000 copies. My book was $9.95 retail, and he wanted a 60% discount."

Unsure of what to do, Diane asked a friend for advice. "She said that if they offered you $20,000 that fast, then they have $40,000. She and I blew the deal. I would have been in the black and I would have had 5,000 books out there for people to say, 'Isn't this adorable? Let's get another copy.' But I didn't understand the premium market back then. It was a rude awakening."

Diane's next big break was landing the Regis and Kathy Lee show. She appeared on the show about nine months after her book came out, and because of that publicity all the book wholesalers were willing to carry *For Popcorn Lovers Only*. During her second year she sold 4,000 copies of her book to Publishers Clearing House. Yet despite her marketing successes she still considered publishing books as more of a hobby than a real business.

"Even though I published my first book in 1987, I didn't get serious about the book industry until 1992. I was still doing commercials and voice-overs, stuff like that. It was about three years before I started pulling in serious money from publishing.

"My start-up costs for Strawberry Patch were about $20,000," Diane cautions. "People can't come into this business having to make money right away — forget it. I had capital saved up, and my husband and I were used to being self-employed. We knew how that works."

Developing a List

Diane's publishing company, Strawberry Patch, has a list with seventeen titles. "I've written six cookbooks, my husband and I have co-written three funny baby books and one marriage book, and I acquired a company with seven titles in 1997 from a lady who had gotten tired of the business." Since Diane's books are very whimsical and kooky, she thought this other line would broaden her market.

"I knew her line of books because we had been doing cooperative mailings together to gift shops. Her books had an elegant, Victorian-type look. She had a real pretty *Write Your Own Cookbook* title, a grandparents' memory journal, and a civil war journal."

The timing for Diane to almost double her number of titles wasn't perfect. "I was having my second baby at age forty-five, but I wanted this lady's sales outlets. She had a lot of big customers for her book like Bed, Bath and Beyond and The Container Store, plus a lot of big chains in the South. I thought it would be a piece of cake."

However, because of the other lady's loss of enthusiasm for the business, she had let things slide for a few years before Diane bought the rights to her titles. "Her big customers had given up on her books by that point, so it took me a while to build her business back up."

Overall, though, Diane is pleased with her decision. "It's not something I would recommend unless you really know a market. And the new titles should be like your titles, but fill a different niche. Then it's fine.

"I write very targeted books like *Gone With the Grits*. When you see that book you know exactly what its market is. This other lady's books are more mass market, like *With Love From My Kitchen*. Anyone could say, 'That is really pretty. My daughter is getting married, and I'd like to get that and put my recipes in it for her.' I was always afraid of books like that because I couldn't feel how to market them. But these books are fun because they've allowed me to get into bigger catalogs since they are kind of generic."

Another of the new titles became Diane's biggest single sale. "There is a company called Reading's Fun out of Iowa that goes into schools and corporations. They set up sales tables in the lobby or lunchrooms, and people come down to buy books at lunch-time. Reading's Fun gives their customers a huge discount, so a publisher has to sell to them at a discount of 80%. They tested a book called *Write Your Own Cookbook* for over a year, and then ordered 90,000 copies." Even with the steep discount, Diane was thrilled. "By printing 90,000 copies I was able to get them below my regular cost."

Diane added extra books to the print run for herself and put together a special mailing to her gift store customers. "I put in something like, 'Hurry, free book offer,' and a little scan of the book cover on the outside of the envelope. I mailed it in October, and inside it said, 'Last minute holiday offer, free book with $75 order.' It was one of the best mailings I have ever done, just great. The book retails for $18.95 so the shop owners were going, wow, I just got a free $20.00 book, and I was happy because I got extra orders."

Though she sold in quantity to Reading's Fun, Diane wouldn't do a similar deal with a discount club like Sam's Club or Costco. "That would really take away from my gift shop sales, and it's not worth it to sell that many books on a returnable basis. I wasn't worried about Reading's Fun because the sale was non-returnable and because they do personal sales to people inside a company or a school for just a couple of days."

Refining the List

Though adding titles has proven beneficial overall, Diane would like to reduce the size of her list. "I would like to get the list down to what is really moving, the titles where I can get volume printings done. I want to keep my print runs at around 10,000 because that's where I can get a good price break. Our books are usually priced at $9.95. If I do a 1,000 or 2,000 printing, there isn't much margin any more. Some books have done their time. Their sales just kind of keep slowing down."

Even so, some books have a way of springing back to life. "In the fall of 1998 I told my husband that this was it for the popcorn book. It had been eleven years, and I was only selling something like 800 copies a year. It was my first book and I didn't do anything standard. It's an odd size and a bit expensive to print. I've sold probably 40,000 copies altogether, but it's never been one of my big sellers.

"Just about the time I said that, they replayed a show on the Discovery channel that I had taped in the spring and had kind of forgotten about. It played three times in November and December, and we got about 500 orders before Christmas."

Diane knows two of her books are dead for sure. "I have a country song book, *Stand by Your Pan*. It took off like bullets, sold and sold and sold, and just kind of pooped out. I probably sold 40,000 copies, but it had a natural up and down. I also did an angel cookbook that was great fun and very profitable. It worked because that angel craze was happening. That was absolutely the easiest book I have marketed in my life."

Some of Diane's books never were good sellers. "One of the books I acquired is the *Civil War Gentleman's Planner*. But guys don't write things down that much. And I wrote a real cute marriage book, but the problem was, who was going to buy it as a gift? It's something that needs to be given to a bridal couple and put in a wedding basket. I deal with a ton of gift basket businesses, and they don't put things like that in their baskets. My general gift stores don't really care for it as a gift. It's one of those books that didn't work."

Another book that didn't do well for Diane was a computer lover's cookbook. "When I wrote the book a few years ago the computer market was still mostly male, and cooking is a female market. Of course there are exceptions, but if you mix markets that don't go together, a book doesn't sell.

"Of the ten books I wrote, the problem with the ones that didn't sell particularly well, the marriage book and the computer cookbook, was that I didn't think about three questions. Who was going to buy them, where were they going to buy them, and could I get the books to those places? If you can truthfully answer those questions, then you have a pretty good idea of whether to pursue an idea."

One of Diane's perennial top selling titles, *Gone With the Grits*, easily passes these three marketing questions. "I can say who is going to buy this book. People who love grits, and people who hate grits and think it's funny. Plus people who have never heard of grits and want to take something home that is southern. Plus people who want to give it to a Yankee as a joke.

"Where are they going to find it? At southern hotels and restaurants, airports, and highway gift shops. I could get the book to those places."

Refreshing an Old Title

Though sales of *Gone With the Grits* have been steady, Diane decided to try something different to make the title seem new again. She came up with the idea of a gourmet grits biscuit that could be sold in the same stores that already carried the book. "I tested it with four to five buyers who I knew would really put in some big orders if they liked it. In the beginning I called it Grits Bits Cookies, but one lady said she absolutely would not carry them if the packaging said cookies. I said okay, how about biscuits?"

Diane hired a woman named Paula Chance to do the packaging design. "I gave her a very strange set of specifications. I said it had to be able to sell in a country type store or in Neiman Marcus, and it had to go with my book. Good luck, honey. She came up with this package that is too cool. You could picture it in Jones' Old Country Store and at the high end of Neiman's shelf.

"I have to sell like a million ounces of these biscuits because the margin is absolutely pathetic compared to the book industry. The book and the biscuits aren't packaged together, so people can still buy them separately, but when people saw them at the gift show where I introduced the biscuits, they bought the book when they bought the biscuits. They look like they go together."

Diane learned about food manufacturing from the wholesale baker who is doing her grits biscuits. "He is absolutely a fountain of information. He is like the Dan Poynter of the gourmet cookie field. I can call him up and ask him, 'What does it mean when a grocery store wants dadada, how do I do this?' He is my payback for all the advice I've given to people about publishing."

The baker erred, though, in his $20,000 estimate of how much it would cost Diane to get her biscuit business up and running. It was closer to $7,000. "He scared me a little bit with what he thought it would cost, but he was considering that I was going to have to do marketing and trade shows, and I already had that in place.

"This was one of the first times I have followed the advice to stay in your market and keep going back to your old customers. I like to develop different markets so if one goes sour I haven't lost my whole customer base, but the problem is it's very expensive finding those markets every time. So this is the first time I have used a market that already existed for me, the southern souvenir market."

In order to make trade shows more affordable, Diane has shared booths in the past, and she has also asked for distressed booths. "Booths run about $2,000, and you've got to have a pretty doggone good show to justify spending $2,000. I ask, 'Do you have any booths you don't know what to do with because they are an odd size or they are by a pole or something?'

"One lady had a long skinny booth. Instead of being 10X10, it was 15X3, but it was all frontage. I didn't need depth, all I needed was for people to see what was on my front table. I got almost the equivalent of 1 1/2 booths for half price. All the other vendors were asking me how I got it. I just asked for a crummy booth and it turned out great."

The Strawberry Patch customer list hovers at around 5,000 names. "It comes and goes. I pare it down by cutting people who haven't ordered in a long time, though I usually keep them for quite a while. It was at about 8,000, but I got really picky and got it down to people who buy pretty frequently."

Bookstores Versus Specialty Sales

Diane sells quite a few books through bookstores, but that is her least favorite market. "I think that part of this business is insane. The only time I pursue bookstores is when I know I am getting coverage in some major press. When I knew that *Southern Living* magazine was going to do an article, I beefed up my calls to some southern bookstores. But I have had too many times when the stores put in a book order too late after a TV show, and then they all come back as returns.

"If they came back in good enough condition that I could sell them, I wouldn't care, but they come back damaged. I don't see how people can run a business if they keep getting messed up books shipped back to them." Diane much prefers the gift store and premium market, where sold books stay sold.

"My focus is to get unusual sales. I like really big sales that reduce my per book costs so I can sell to my mom and pop stores on a better margin. If I can nail a couple of really big things like the Reading's Fun deal, that helps me because then I am selling a $2.00 book to the gift shops instead of one that cost me $5.00."

Premium sales, though, are unpredictable. "You can't bank on these deals because they are very fluky. It's like fishing when you land a great big one out of nowhere. They don't follow any particular rhyme or reason."

A deal that Diane did with Quaker Oats shows the value of persistence when pursuing the premium market. "I went after them for four years. I went through about ten different brand managers during that time. I would think I had somebody close to a deal, then boom, they would leave the company or change departments, and I would have to start all over again.

"I had pretty much given up, but one night a lady called me and said, 'I am the new brand manager. We are getting ready to retool our packaging and we are interested in your *Grits* cookbook.'

"That was it. Quaker wanted to buy 15,000 copies and put a coupon for the book on sixteen million boxes of Quaker grits. They wanted a 65% discount, but I never had to touch their copies. I just called my printer and said print 25,000. Send them 15,000 and I'll take the other 10,000. And of course my print costs were low. It was wonderful."

In 1999 Diane cemented another sizeable sale. "I made a premium deal to a catalog for 65,000 copies of the same book Reading's Fun had bought, *With Love From My Kitchen*. That sale raised my annual sales volume to $325,000."

Publicity

"Print reviews in magazines and newspapers are the most important facet of promotions, more than TV shows or anything like that. Print seems to hang around a lot longer. A TV show creates an immediate impulse, but then people forget. With print, they will cut something out and keep it. They may put it down, but later they pick it up again. Print media produces sales over a longer time period."

Diane doesn't do a lot of prepublication publicity. "I don't do galleys, and I don't send anything to *Publishers Weekly*. But I will send a cookbook and a press release to at least 200 food editors. If there is any kind of occasion coming up like National Popcorn Month or something like that, I'll send out postcards.

"I really love TV because it's very targeted. There are only so many places you can be on. I only do the big syndicated shows and maybe some shows locally. I don't travel around the country doing every morning show. That doesn't work when I've got little ones at home. Anyway, it's not necessary.

"I've gotten very lazy about radio the last couple of years. For some reason radio just doesn't pay off for me. I would do radio shows just as cute as I could, and every time do them the same way, but sometimes the phone wouldn't stop ringing and sometimes it wouldn't ring one time. I know it's great to get my name out there, but I got bored with radio interviews."

Combining Motherhood with Publishing

"I didn't know I was going to get married and have kids because I did it so late in my life. I got married the same year I came out with my first book, and I had my first baby a year later at age thirty-eight. Then I had my second at age forty-five.

Diane would still work uncounted hours a week like she did when she was single, but her life doesn't allow those kind of hours anymore. "Because I am older and have a young family, I had to get really clear with myself. What's fun? What's interesting? I have done things just to do them, but now I make sure I have a passion for each book that I do. I thought about doing a Beanie Baby cookbook when that was so hot, but it didn't really interest me.

"It's been probably 75% of my enjoyment of this business that I can do both, be a mother and a publisher. I have the ability to get up at dawn and do most of my business before the kids wake up. I work about five hours a day during the week, and on weekends I work a couple of hours before the kids get up."

Diane knows that she's cramming a lot into her life, but she's satisfied. "I feel that if anything happened to me tomorrow, you would be hard pressed to find anyone to say, 'Poor thing, she never got to do anything.' You would have to look hard to find a broad who did more in the past ten years than I have. While I would never deny it's not an easy thing to have little ones around and work, I feel real tickled to have been able to have all of this."

Chapter Seven

Success on a Shoestring

Starting a successful business with almost no money is the stuff of legend. The reality is many undercapitalized businesses fail. Cheri Thurston, a teacher looking for an alternative career, beat the odds.

"I was a teacher for many years," Cheri explains. "I loved teaching, but I became one of those people who burn out eventually. Most of my experience is at the junior high school level, and although that was my favorite, it was very demanding. I never found a way to teach that didn't consume me."

Cheri started to explore other career options. "I kept looking for something else to do. A big influence on me was a book called *Wishcraft: How to Get What You Really Want* by Barbara Sher. She said to do something tomorrow toward reaching your dream, but I couldn't figure out what my dream might be."

Cheri was also used to being her own boss. "As a teacher, as long as you do a good job and handle your own problems, you can do what you want." Plus Cheri loved writing. One of the books she was reading suggested selling something via the mail, and that appealed to her.

"The book said that a mail order business was something you could start with little money. I had been recently divorced, and I had absolutely no money. I hit on the idea of writing books that I wished I had as a teacher. I always wrote my own material for my kids because I had a disdain for most school textbooks.

There wasn't a lot of material available for junior high school students then. People expected teachers to use elementary material or to dumb down high school material, but junior high kids are a really different age. I wanted to write material that was targeted to that age group."

Cheri wrote two books, *Cottonwood Game Book: Surviving Last Period and Other Desperate Situations* and *Cottonwood Composition Book: When They Think That They Have Nothing to Write About*. "These are very practical books. The teachers can photocopy them and use them in class tomorrow. They have a sense of humor and I know they work with kids because they are materials that I used."

In order to conserve her money, Cheri didn't start off with bound books to sell. "I was so cautious. A friend lent me $2,000 to start Cottonwood Press. I printed only the covers because I had a sense that how things looked was important and I wanted the books to look professional, but I didn't have the guts to actually print the books because it would have taken too much money."

She waited until she received some orders, then went to a local printing place and photocopied the inside of the books. "I would do 10-20 books at a time. I would take these nicely done covers with me and the printer would put the plastic comb binding on the books."

Cheri is glad she started small. "It was a blessing. I highly recommend doing it this way. I made mistakes like everyone does, but they were on a smaller scale. I remember someone who was going into business about the same time I was who had a lot of funding compared to me. He is no longer around, but I am. I think the mistakes he made hurt a lot more because they were on a larger scale."

Cheri sold her books on the side for a little over a year. "I was still teaching and the next summer I wrote more books. I went back to teaching part-time that fall, but by October I knew I had to quit something." Cheri expected a bad reaction to her desire to break her teaching contract, but her colleagues surprised her with their support. "They all said if you don't make it you can come back. People were so nice.

"I had a hard time the first few years. I had a credit card that I used too much. A lot of times people would say, 'Do you want to go out for breakfast?' and I would say, 'Let me check the mail first to see if I got any money.'

"I remember at one point a bunch of friends all brought over care baskets. They were joking about it, but it was appreciated. I was never in danger of starving to death, but it was nice. Though things were hard for a long time, I have never once regretted it."

By her second year Cheri had four or five books in print, all of them written by her. She sometimes used pen names to make it look like several authors had written the books. "I have so many names that I never know who I am," Cheri jokes, who has remarried and uses yet another name socially. "It's very funny at times."

Cheri also started a newsletter called the *Cottonwood Monthly*. "That was how I started buying materials written by other people. We paid, but it wasn't very much, I think about $25. For the authors it was their break into print. Putting out the newsletter was grueling. Someone offered to buy it some years ago, and I sold it."

Hiring Staff

In the meantime Cheri acquired her first employee. "A college student called me and said she was so interested in publishing that she would do an internship for nothing while she was going to school. This was around '90 or '91. I was working out of my bedroom in a little tiny house, so I met her for coffee. Any meetings I did at that time were out of the coffee shop."

Cheri hadn't planned on hiring someone so soon. "She volunteered to work for nothing, so I took her on. As soon as I could, I started paying her something. Having her really helped my sanity more than anything. It becomes obvious at some point that you have to do something. You can't write, you can't fill orders, you can't do everything yourself, at least I couldn't. I got some help that I greatly needed at that point."

Cheri still struggles with the issues involved in growing a company and adding employees. "I have seven full and part-time employees, and I am less and less able to get to the things that I am good at doing. I need to spend my time writing and editing, and what I'm doing is administrative stuff, putting out fires here and there. Emptying my in-basket has become almost a full time job sometimes.

"I operate a very open kind of business because that is my philosophy, but still, nobody else gets the big picture. I am the only one who knows all of the details. Even though I think I am pretty good at delegating, some things I just can't. I haven't found anybody who can do the writing and the editing. People can do different stages of it, but I still have to go over it."

Cottonwood Press is now run out of an office building instead of Cheri's home. "We have an average of three to four new books each year. In 1998 we came out with some different products and didn't do a book. We published three books in 1999. I would have liked to have done five, but we moved two of them to January, 2000."

With over 35 titles in print, picking and packing books for shipment is a sizeable task. "We have stacks of books going out the door every day. Order fulfillment is a large part of two people's jobs. I also have two people to do book design and graphics, though I have moved from having an in-house artist to farming that out to different artists."

Though she's no longer officially a teacher, Cheri's natural bent comes out with her employees. "One thing I find interesting is that the staff, none of whom were writers, have ended up becoming writers. People's talents get developed here, and I feel good about that. We did a book a couple of years ago which was called *A Month of Fundays-a whole year of games and activities for just about every holiday you've ever heard of - and many that you haven't.* I think that it is one of our best books, and it was completely staff written. Everybody submitted ideas and we had hundreds and hundreds of things that we kept working with until we ended up with a really good book.

"I always wish I could pay my staff more, but they all know I will pay them as well as I can and offer other benefits, like being flexible with hours. Everybody feels like they own the company and is as proud of every success we have as I am. I hire totally on my instincts and on nothing else. My philosophy is to hire people who are real smart and literate. They don't have to know what they will eventually have to know for the job. They do have to be able to figure things out, and they must be honest."

Trying Out Unusual Material

One of Cheri's early titles was a book of poetry that dealt with teaching called *Hide Your Ex-Lax Under the Wheaties.* "There are funny poems and poignant ones. I had been working on it for years, and it's done really well. Lots of people use it in workshops and college education classes and for teacher education. I won an honorable mention in the Colorado Book Awards for that book. We've sold over 5,000 copies since 1994. I don't know how many I sold before then because my records are stored in boxes in my basement."

Besides books, Cottonwood Press produces posters and a CD-ROM. "We just came out with a line of Parts of Speech posters. This sounds so boring, but they are really funny. They are all based on pictures from the fifties, a kind of retro look. People love them. Then we have a set of posters that we call How to Pass, How to Flunk. Teachers just stand around roaring when they read them; they just fly off the shelf."

Cheri dragged her feet when it came to getting into software. "I always know which books are going to sell a lot. I always know the ones that are going to be the best. When we turned a book into a CD-ROM, I felt uneasy. I didn't think it was going to take off, and sure enough it hasn't. It's a great CD, but it doesn't sell in the same way our books do.

"We haven't acquired a wholesaler for the CD-ROM, and it hasn't been a good seller through our catalog even though the people who have bought it have really praised it. I can't say it was a mistake because I think we needed to do it to see what that's all about, but I'm not rushing to try another CD-ROM version of one of our books anytime soon!"

Even though Cheri knows it might be wisest to focus on her core market, sometimes she just can't resist publishing something that doesn't fit with the rest of her products. "My goal in life is not to be rich, but to do what I want. And to have enough money to do it if I want to do it. If there is anything I have learned in this business it is that first you figure out what you want to do, then you figure out a way to go do it. There is always some way to do some part of what you want to do.

"Anyway, I had a friend who was a director of a senior adult education class at Aims Community College. She told me about a woman who taught an autobiography writing class called Writing Your Life. I went and observed a class because the idea intrigued me. I loved the class, and I decided we needed to do a book on it. *Writing Your Life: An Easy-to-Follow Guide to Writing an Autobiography*, became a finalist in the Benjamin Franklin Awards contest in 1990 in its first version, and the new version is far better. It is probably my favorite book."

Despite Cheri's enthusiasm for the title, she put no money into promoting it because it didn't fit her line of products. However, it still did well. "I got a review in the *The Rocky Mountain News*. We sent out copies to anyone who might do something with it.

"The person who was the director at Aims now works for me. She knows a lot of people and she'll say, 'Take a look at this book.' Or she'll see someone doing a newsletter about biography writing so she'll give them some information. Or else she'll suggest they do some classes for senior adults and we'll give a discount on the book. They get a class going and it works amazingly well."

Bottom Line PERSONAL magazine has twice given *Writing Your Life* a plug in the month of December. "One of my employees, Susan, said I ought to look at getting into this magazine. They wrote a nice little plug. We had a lot of orders from that. We had to throw something in for the customer so we didn't charge shipping. It was totally free publicity, which was great. On most of our books, though, we can't even try for that kind of publicity because our material is designed for teachers, not the general market."

Inventory Dilemmas

Cottonwood Press has sold around 10,000 copies of *Writing Your Life* in the past ten years. Reprints usually consist of 1,000-2,000 copies. "Our normal print run quantities depend on the title, anywhere between 1,000 to 7,000. The 7,000 print run is an odd one. It's for a book called *My Personal Yearbook*, and we have to print the book in large quantities to get the price low enough for teachers to buy classroom sets. We do print runs of 3,000-4,000 for our best selling books.

"My old philosophy was to print no more copies than I would use in a year. Now I'm trying to cut down the size of our print runs because inventory is a huge problem. Every square inch of the office is filled with books. My office has a little wall down part of it and behind that wall are books, and they are also in every corner. We find ways to kind of hide them. One room is just stuffed with them."

Besides space issues, Cheri has run into a problem capitalizing her inventory. Though she used to be able to fund new books with the profits from the increasing sales of her backlist books, her sales increases have leveled off, primarily because she can't increase her marketing budget every year. "It's a cash flow problem. When I can't increase the number of catalogs we send out, sales stay about the same. Yet I have to pay for adding new books in order to keep our old customers coming back. I have discontinued one book and am thinking about discontinuing another one only because I can't afford to keep reprinting them. This is a huge problem. I sometimes don't have the cash to pay the bills because my money is sitting in inventory.

"It's tough. I don't want to discontinue books, but at the same time I have some really good new books that I want to print. I am going to have to discontinue some books to make room for the new ones. I am struggling with this issue right now."

Uneven Cash Flow Pattern

Part of Cheri's cash flow problem comes from her market. "I've seen a huge change over the years. Our customer used to be a teacher spending her own money to buy one or two books. As we added new titles, we got more purchase orders from school districts because the teachers wanted several books and they wanted the school districts to pay for them.

"This switch has changed the time of year that the big orders come in. Our worst month used to be July, and now it is our best. But we get no money in July because no one is in school to pay the bills. So the school purchase orders come in, we have put all this money into printing the books, and we don't get paid until October or November. The good thing is we have no collection problems because the schools always pay. It just may take them a while."

Cheri accidentally stumbled upon a way to partially even out her cash flow. "I was talking with a friend and it came up that I play accordion. She said she didn't know this about me, so I said I'd have to come out of the closet. It struck a chord and I came up with the idea of forming an organization, Closet Accordion Players of America. I wrote a funny press release and sent it out to 40-50 newspapers around the county."

The media loved the idea. Cheri's organization has been featured in almost every major newspaper in the country including *USA Today*. "It's gotten to the point that I don't send out press releases in June anymore, which is National Accordion Awareness Month, because I'm so tired of doing the radio interviews. I can't keep up with them. It's hysterical. Talk about free publicity, not for my company, but for this $12.95 membership."

The membership includes a newsletter four times a year. Membership renewals arrive year round, but especially in the month of June. "It sort of helps even out the income around here, and it's something I like doing. Plus you know how a lot of companies do these rope courses and things to build team work and spirit? Well, we have accordion lessons. Each one of the staff gets six months of free accordion lessons. One woman who is fifty-three had never played a musical instrument in her life. She learned to play, and she is so proud of herself. This is part of what leads to a feeling of comraderie around here. We are supportive of one another."

Adding Other Authors

"We get lots and lots of manuscripts in the mail, most of them nothing at all like what we do at Cottonwood Press. I have this file called Amazingly Bad Stuff. In the file there's a book of tattoo designs, a book of religious games for three-year-olds, things that are wildly inappropriate for us.

"We are looking for creative materials. I don't believe in mindless busy work or writing to readability formulas that dumb things down for kids. I want clear writing that makes the kids think and use their creativity, material with a sense of humor. Our target audience is 7th, 8th, and 9th grade, though we say our materials are for 5th through 12th because people use them all over the spectrum.

"I think our first book by someone else is our current best seller, *Hot Fudge Monday: Tasty Ways to Teach Parts of Speech to Students Who Have a Hard Time Swallowing Anything to Do with Grammar.* In that case, the author, Randy Larson, did everything exactly right. He wrote a query letter to me that was literate, funny and even praised my materials, pointing out that he used them in his classroom.

"But what proved he was right for us was the material he sent. As my mother said at the time, 'I can't tell if you wrote this or if he did.' We hashed out a deal and ended up with two books out of the first manuscript he sent me. I offered him a contract without having the complete book, which is unheard of around here because we usually need to see the whole thing. He had done his research and his homework. He is really great and he has continued to write things for us."

Cheri is open to receiving submissions from other writers if their material matches both the Cottonwood Press focus on teaching materials and the company's tone. "People who read our stuff say the writers must really know kids. They must have been in the classroom." Cheri recommends that hopeful authors read some of Cottonwood's books before they send anything, but realizes they will seldom pay attention. "Virtually no one believes this advice. Just because we do education books, authors think all educational materials will fit us, but they don't."

Because of requests from teachers, Cheri is thinking about branching out from English materials into math and science. "It would be a big departure for us, but teachers want materials like our current stuff in these other areas. I would especially like to get submissions for math."

Breaking the Rules

In some areas Cheri has decided to do things differently than what is considered to be the right way, particularly in the area of covers and binding. "I think that a lot of the rules you hear about in some of the publishing classes fit books sold through bookstores. They don't fit us. Early on I did one-color covers and a one-color catalog, which by the way had a fantastic response, but people would tell us we needed to have a book that was full color. But why do that when I'm advertising that book in a one-color catalog? And the teachers don't care because they are going to copy the activity sheets."

Cheri binds some of her books with spiral binding. "People all over the country who teach told us they wanted spiral binding. They love it. They can lay it flat on the copy machine and it doesn't fall apart. But everyone says spiral binding is a real no-no because I'll lose bookstore sales. So? I'm not going after that market. I agree with Dan Poynter, I think it was, who says that bookstores are the worst place to sell books."

Not following the industry "rules" leads to problems whenever Cheri enters her books in publisher book contests. "I am trying not to enter many of our books in contests anymore because they just make me mad. The comments are so inappropriate or silly. One judge marked us down for using dark brown for the hot fudge sauce on the cover of *Hot Fudge Monday*. He thought chocolate brown was a bad color choice for a book.

"Another judge said we were not being sensitive to color blind people because a book cover had a lot of purple and red in it. Give me a break. What about people with dyslexia, or people who can't read at all? Are we supposed to design covers with them in mind, too? There are limits, I think, to what we should consider when designing a book cover."

Direct Marketing Her Books

Cheri's initial marketing consisted of sending out a flyer to a list of 1,000 names that she bought. That flyer has been transformed over the years into a catalog. "The vast majority of our sales are from direct catalogs that go out to teachers all over the country, or by word of mouth. Our mailing list is about 15,000 names.

"Our direct sales have leveled off, though. I was concerned about that, but then I saw an increase in our distributor sales." Cheri defines distributors quite broadly, including in that category the other catalogs that carry her products. "I think many of our customers are now buying from these cataloguers, and that might account for some of the leveling. There is less money per title, but it's nice to sell to distributors. When you get the check it's much bigger than when you get an order for three books from a teacher."

In addition to receiving less money per book, the other downside to selling a higher percentage of her books through various distributors is the loss of contact with teachers. Cheri tries to make up for this by attending conferences. "I like to be in touch so we know what is working and how they feel. We always listen for new ideas.

"We don't do a lot of conferences. Most of the state ones are too small. It doesn't pay to go unless they are nearby and expenses are low. We go to national and regional language arts and middle school conferences. Language arts and middle school conferences anywhere in Colorado, Texas, and California are usually good, too.

"Oddly enough, the conferences occur in clumps. In 1999 the four big conferences that we usually go to in the spring were all held on the same weekend. It was hard to cover all of them, as well as the office, especially because we had one pregnant person who couldn't travel and two people with small children. I wound up getting my sister out of school to help, and a friend in Washington recruited her sister. Even pulling in these extra people, we still had to cancel one conference. We normally do about 10-12 conferences between September and May. It's expensive to attend."

Cheri does very little advertising besides listings in the backs of her books. "I read Dan Poynter's book and even went to his class. He pretty much said don't advertise and I paid attention. I did try ads here and there a little bit, and he was right. I found almost all of them worthless."

The exception for her was running an ad in *The English Journal*. "It is targeted to my audience. The advertising was fairly inexpensive so I could do a half page for a reasonable amount. I would track the sales. The ads always resulted in sales equalling about three times the cost of the ad."

Going OnLine

Cottonwood Press participates in the Amazon Advantage Program. "I am surprised. Amazon.com is selling quite a few of our books. We get orders every other day or so, ten, twenty, or more books at a time."

Cheri hesitated about doing a web site for Cottonwood Press. "It seemed like a stretch to me. We've had it for a couple of years and I think it is worth it. We had a guy working for us who did any computer stuff that had to be done. He pushed us into it. I kept dragging my feet, not thinking it could ever be a good idea. But it was. Whereas in the beginning we got orders once every couple of weeks, now we get orders on the web every day.

"I also think a web site lends us a certain legitimacy. We get a lot of calls from people who found us on the web, thought our site looked interesting, and wanted a catalog. We also actually published a book by someone who found us on the web."

Bookstores

The bookstore market is responsible for a very small percentage of Cottonwood's sales, but those sales are the most frustrating for Cherie. "Bookstores come to us for special orders. A few bookstores around the country that are teacher bookstores carry all of our stuff, and so does the Tattered Cover in Denver. We make very little money through bookstores. I hate dealing with them, probably because I don't know how to handle things correctly. It's more aggravating than lucrative."

It's not the bookstores in particular that bother Cheri, but rather the wholesalers that sell to them. "I have never figured out how to deal with them effectively. One day they are returning nine books and the next day we get an order for those same nine books. Now we send them half of what they ask for. That seems to work. We don't get nearly the number of returns anymore."

Producing a Catalog

Cottonwood Press experimented with the format and size of one of their most recent catalogs, and Cheri was disappointed with the results. "There wasn't too much text, just too much text compared to the image space. The proportion became unbalanced."

The sales for some books dropped off somewhat, but that didn't worry Cheri. "We could account for that by the space we gave them in the catalog and the placement. I knew if I put them in a different position and gave them more play the following year, then they would do fine."

Some books sell more poorly than they should because of their titles. "I have a title I wish I had changed before printing," Cheri laments. "It was *Homework is Not Another Word for Something Else to Lose*. It's about helping students who want to succeed in school and setting them up for success. We have this gimmick which is funny titles, and it usually works. However, the mistake I made with this one is that teachers see the word 'homework' and think it's a bunch of homework activities. If they aren't looking for homework activities, they skip reading about the book. The book isn't about homework at all, so the title is misleading."

Sales for this book are picking up, and now Cheri feels that she is stuck with the title because so many people recognize it. "What I might do is experiment a little more with the subtitle. Or I could make the title less prominent and the subtitle bigger. I play around with books like that to make them more successful."

Pricing the Books

"Some publishers are shocked at the prices we can get for our books. A book I sell for $14.95 a big company might sell for only $4.95. The book isn't very long, just 71 pages, but all our books may be reproduced by the teachers to use in their own classroom. That is a selling point. Plus the people who have used our materials before know how well they work with real kids.

"The first book I printed is the same price as it was in the beginning. Our most expensive book is $21.95. I go by my gut on knowing what a teacher will pay for something. It seems to work."

Cheri has also looked at the other end of the price and profit equation. "I've learned how to print books much more economically." But that doesn't mean she always goes with the lowest bid when she selects a printer. "We have had some unpleasant experiences with printers. Some are really bad or hard to work with."

Her favorite printers currently are United Graphics, out of Illinois, and Kendall Printing in Greeley, Colorado. "Kendall is wonderful. They tend to be a little higher than others, but not a lot."

The slightly higher price is offset by good service and the advantages of working with a local printer. "Their quality control is so good. If there is a problem, they fix it. We don't even have to go to them. They come here and pick stuff up, show us proofs, whatever. And they are fast. We always get our books in two weeks."

Advice for Others

Cheri believes small publishers should think for themselves. "I don't think you should pay too much attention to the rules. You should listen to them and see if they fit you, but don't be afraid to break them. You can find books that break all the rules and are wonderful sellers and others that follow all the rules, but don't sell at all.

"Every year I am in this business, I am more and more convinced of the importance of a sense of audience. People don't often have it. You need to know who you are writing for, understand how they are going to see your material and interpret it. You must know what they want. My staff learns this from me and from going to conferences where they talk to our customers. At this point I don't have anyone working for me who is or has been a teacher, but they all feel like they have been.

"You should trust your instincts and then be sensible about it. I don't ever take such wild leaps that I think they might jeopardize my business. I don't think that hugely right brain people would make it as publishers. You need to have a good left brain, right brain split in your skills."

Cheri's financial limitations at the beginning caused her to make some equipment purchasing decisions that she now thinks were not the best. "If I were starting over, I probably wouldn't go with PCs. When I started out, I didn't have money. A Mac seemed a smarter move, but it was just enough more money that I didn't do it. I think Macs would be a better choice for the kind of people who work with me, more user friendly."

Despite the tough years, Cheri is happy about her choice of career. "I do what I want to do. I am working all the time, but I like it. I'm having fun."

Chapter Eight

Transformed from Unpublished Fiction Writer into Hot Author

Like many fiction writers, M.J. Rose wanted to be published by one of the big New York houses. When she finished her first manuscript, *Living the Questions*, she sent it to an agent, just as first-time authors are supposed to do. "Loretta Barrett, the agent I wanted and the first agent who saw it, took it," M. J. says. "I was ecstatic."

Barrett sent the manuscript off to twelve publishing houses. Right away two of them said they were interested in making a deal, but first they had to let their marketing departments take a look. That's where the deals died. "Just because an editor wants a manuscript isn't enough anymore," M. J. explains. "Now the marketing departments have to sign off on books."

Still, M. J. and Barrett were encouraged by the enthusiasm displayed by the editors, so M. J. started to work on a second novel. "Loretta sent out *Lip Service* , and within a few weeks two editors said they loved the story and wanted to publish it."

When the marketing department of the first house read *Lip Service*, though, that deal fell through. "While they felt they could sell 10,000 copies, they weren't sure they could sell 25,000 copies. And that was their standard."

The problem was how *Lip Service* crossed genres: it was both a thriller and an erotic novel. "They'd never had a book quite like it and didn't know how to market it," M. J. explains.

That rejection didn't bother M. J. because the other publishing house had come through with an offer that she and Barrett accepted. Then, at the last minute, a problem surfaced. "When the editorial department of that house realized it was a first novel they reneged. They were a new house and needed to guarantee sales, so they were only buying authors who came with a built-in readership."

M. J. found herself caught in the classic Catch 22. "At that point I stopped writing for a while. Loretta wanted me to write a third novel, but I had some life issues to deal with first; my marriage was in trouble and my mother was terminally ill."

Experimenting with the Internet

After a six-month absence, M. J. began to research a third novel. "I was doing all my research on the Internet. The more time I spent online the more I realized what an amazing marketing potential the Net offered writers. In the bricks and mortar world you have to find your readers. Online, your readers find you. I decided to get a web site to offer *Lip Service* as an electronic download. No one had done anything like that with fiction yet, and I wanted to see what would happen. I wasn't thinking about having a publishing company. I wasn't even thinking about printing the book."

M. J. offered a download version of *Lip Service* for $9.95 and a copied version for $16.00 plus shipping and handling. "I figured nobody would want the hard copy; I just put it up there for the one person who might not want to download the book."

To get attention for the book and to jump start sales, M. J. bought a couple of online direct marketing lists. "I purchased two lists of readers from Postmaster Direct. This is not considered spam because the people on these lists have agreed to get advertising online about subjects they are interested in. The lists were very expensive, but I did start to get orders. The surprise was that for every person who wanted a download, ten wanted a printed version."

M. J. plunged herself into learning about publishing. "I quickly read everything I could about self-publishing, independent publishing, and publishing on the web. I joined PMA and started getting in touch with the printers other PMA members had used."

Getting into Print

M. J. knew she needed a wholesaler, but only the smaller companies were interested. She chose Valentine Publishing Group, a small wholesaler who works with Baker & Taylor.

Because she wanted her book to look professional, M. J. hired a graphic designer to do the cover. "I invested a lot of money on the cover, but research shows the cover sells a book 80% of the time."

M. J. was amazed at how easy it was to get her book into print. "I thought the printing would be the most complicated part, but it was simple compared to marketing. The printer worked directly from my laser copy so there wasn't a typesetting fee. I used Microsoft Word. The only mistake I made in the layout is that the pages weren't right justified. And although I had the book proofread twice, there were still typos."

She spent approximately $7,000 to print 3,000 copies of her book, plus another $1,500 for the cover design and $1,000 to buy the cover art. "The graphic designer, despite her being a friend, charged me full price, but that enabled me to treat her the same as a real supplier. I turned down six covers before I chose four to test market outside a Victoria's Secret store in a Connecticut shopping mall."

Getting Serious about Publicity

Heeding the warnings she had read about advertising being a waste of money, M. J. focused on publicity. Some of the things she tried worked, and others turned out to be a waste of money. Her most expensive mistake was hiring a New York PR company. "They were so excited about the book that they cut their rate, down to 10% of what they normally charge, but it was still a small fortune. They were overly ambitious in what they thought they were going to be able to do in a short period of time, and they were only able to get me one real placement."

In the meantime M. J. had begun to do her own PR and marketing on the web. "I put together a list of over two hundred web sites and e-zines that reached my target audience — women who read and women who felt comfortable with their sexuality. I also joined list servs that reached the same two groups and always included the name of my novel and my web site address in my signature."

In order to start some buzz, M.J. came up with innovative ways to get reviews. "I sent a letter to the PMA list serv saying that if anybody wanted a free copy of the book, I would be happy to send it to them. In exchange, if they liked *Lip Service*, I'd like a review. About twenty-five people asked for the book, including Linda Richards who was the editor of January magazine.

"She wrote a review saying my book read like a more intelligent Danielle Steel. Initially, I was upset because *Lip Service* isn't a romance. But when I realized that Danielle Steel sells billions of books, I figured this review would do great things for my novel."

M. J. sent Richard's review out with the review copies of *Lip Service*, and started to get additional reviews. "Probably my biggest break came when a woman I didn't know contacted me and told me she was reviewing my book. She turned out to be Marcy Sheiner, editor of the Herotica Series and author of the

Joy of Sex. Marcy's starred review was printed in the *San Francisco Spectator*, a sexually oriented newspaper, and that got *Lip Service* more attention."

Although *Lip Service* didn't fit into the standard definition of the romance genre, M. J. knew that many romance readers would enjoy it. As an advertising executive, M. J. had worked with Harlequin books and knew what readers wanted. "I had done focus groups with over five thousand women over a two-year period. These were readers of romance and commercial fiction, and one of the things that stuck with me was how many women use books the way men use *Playboy* and *Penthouse* and X-rated movies."

M. J. decided to take a chance on an ad in *Romantic Times*. "What I got for the price was incredible. Four hundred fifty dollars bought me an audience of 150,000 women who loved to read. Plus there is a lot of pass-along. Many women who subscribe give the magazine to their friends."

Romantic Times ran a four star review of *Lip Service* the same month that M. J.'s ad appeared. "The ad paid for itself. I tracked it by the jump in Amazon.com orders."

In the meantime M. J. continued to spend hours on the web searching for places to promote her book. "I worked six hours a day, six days a week, going to sites that had to do with women, books, erotica or highbrow sexuality. If I thought a site might be interested in reviewing the book or having me write an article for them, I would send them a letter. I realized that because *Lip Service* was erotic and literate, it would stand out."

Looking back, M. J. can see where she could have cut corners. "The $10,000 for the PR firm was a total waste of money. The $1,000 to set up a credit card merchant account on my site was ridiculous — all I needed to do was sell the book through Amazon.com. Plus I did some things backwards. I shouldn't have done any promotion until I had the reviews for the book.

"The biggest mistake I made was being impatient. But I was at a time in my life where so many bad things had happened, and

I needed a good thing to happen. If I had taken a little more time to read — or if there were a book available like the one I later wrote with Angela Adair-Hoy, *The Secrets of Our Success*, I could have saved myself $15,000."

A Really Good Thing Happens

Just as M. J. was beginning to think she had tapped out the web's promotional opportunities, she received an e-mail from Erika Tsang, an editor with Doubleday Book Club and the Literary Guild. Tsang had come across *Lip Service*'s reviews at Amazon.com, and she asked for a copy of the novel. Two weeks later M. J. became the first self-published fiction author to have her novel selected by a major book club. She was also the first novelist to be discovered online.

Suddenly *Lip Service* became a hot property. M. J.'s agent organized an auction for the rights to *Lip Service*, and in an author's dream come true, almost a dozen publishing houses asked for copies to read. The rights ended up being sold to PocketBooks, a division of Simon & Schuster.

"Just walking into the Simon & Schuster building as an author was more exciting than anything else that happened," M. J. admits. "They had seven people waiting to meet me from all the departments, including the head of publicity. They were thrilled about the book and wanted to talk about how I had done this crazy thing. One of the things we discussed was how with a fiction title there is rarely any news for the press, but with *Lip Service* they had a Cinderella story."

M. J. still had over a thousand copies of her first printing of *Lip Service*, but fortunately her new publisher bought 500 copies to use in place of galleys. M. J.'s high five-figure advance erased any regrets she had about any leftover copies.

Foreign rights weren't included as part of the deal with Pocket Books, and the total amount of advances for foreign rights deals soon exceeded the advance for the domestic rights. "We've sold foreign rights to England, Australia, France, Germany and the Netherlands," said M. J.

What Happened After the Sale

During the following eight months articles about M. J. appeared in *Forbes*, *Time*, *New York Magazine*, *Newsweek*, *The LA Times*, *The New York Times*, *Business 2.0 Magazine*, and *The Industry Standard*. She also appeared on *"The Today Show"* and *"Fox News Five"*. Relieved of the promotional duties that had previously been her responsibility as her own publisher, M. J. had the time to write a new novel, *In Fidelity*. Pocket Books bought the domestic rights to that title, too.

Following the publicity around the sale of *Lip Service*, M. J. received over 1,000 letters from writers wanting help. M. J. teamed up with co-author Angela Adair-Hoy to write an e-book called *The Secrets of Our Success — How to Publish and Promote Online*. "The book was only the second e-book to be reviewed by *Publishers Weekly*," M. J. says. "It also became the second e-book to sell to the Doubleday Book Club and The Literary Guild as a featured alternate selection."

Advice for Fiction Writers

"It's harder for fiction writers to get published by a big house than for non-fiction writers," M. J. states sympathetically. "I think it was the editors who originally wanted to buy my novels who gave me the courage to self-publish.

"If I hadn't gotten so close with those NY houses I don't know if I would have tried self-publishing *Lip Service*. As a fiction writer I would be nervous about publishing a book until I had serious evaluation from objective professionals."

M. J. believes more authors will take to the web to try out their books on the public. "I'd recommend that authors test market their books online as e-books. It's a brave new world out there and a very exciting time for writers."

Chapter Nine

A Job She Can Take with Her

Bonnie Marlewski-Probart has moved ten times during the nine years she's been married. "It hampers my ability to expand into new markets when I'm never sure where I'm going to be," Bonnie says. "Although my choice of direction would be to move out of the horse industry and into a more mainline market, I've chosen the easy route and stayed in the niche market."

Because Bonnie's husband is an extremely well paid contract worker, her publishing company, K & B Products, is their number two work priority. "It's economics, not that I'm some weak female. My husband makes an obscene amount of money so my business comes second. I always have to be prepared to lock the door and move somewhere else." Bonnie is also the partner in the marriage who calls the movers, packs their belongings, and finds a new home to rent or buy. "I can only pay part-time attention to my job."

Despite these limitations, Bonnie usually clears over $20,000 per year with her publishing business. Most of her income comes from book sales, though she also teaches writing classes for community colleges and does about ten speaking engagements a year. "I would like to do more speaking, but it's got to be worth it. I don't book small potato gigs, only big ones."

From Owner of a Horse Farm to Freelance Writer

When Bonnie graduated from high school she took a job with Mobil Oil Corporation. "At the end of my fifth year, a woman from the human resources department told me I would be pleased to know that in a few years I would be fully vested in the retirement program. She said it like it was supposed to be good news, but a cold chill ran down my back. I thought, 'Am I going to die here working for some yahoo corporation?'" Professionally trained as a rider since she was a girl, Bonnie eventually decided to quit her job and buy a horse farm in Indiana. It was her dream at that time, and she didn't want to miss her chance to make it happen.

"At the farm I was teaching lessons, training horses, and going to horse shows. I stayed there for five years through killer winters and hot summers," Bonnie says. "Running a storefront business has got to be the hardest business on the planet."

Tired of the horse farm hassles, Bonnie left the farm and started doing freelance articles. "I started out writing for horse markets because that was what I knew. I had intense hands-on experience, and knew what I did worked. When editors turned me down there was no question of whether or not the material sucked. The problem was how I wrote."

Bonnie soon learned how to produce quality work that suited the demographics of each magazine. "There are a million reasons why articles get turned down, and only one has anything to do with what you wrote. I learned to study the demographics of a magazine and be very clear about who the reader was. Then I would understand exactly what the editor needed in terms of types of material. I would deliver great information in a language that was clearly understandable by that magazine's readers.

"I think what stops most people from being successful as freelancers is they somehow think writing has something to do with them. Everybody will want to read about me and my reality. But it's about the customer, the reader. When I started writing freelance, I used the same attitude I had when I taught riding. If I put you on a horse, and you can't understand a concept, it's my fault. If you're coming to me to learn, and I can't teach you on a level you can understand, that's my fault.

"Because I don't write fiction, everything I do is very how to, matter-of-fact, let me help you solve a problem. I write with the voice of the demographic I'm targeting. Say I'm writing for a woman's magazine with a 35-45 year-old female reader who has 2.5 kids and a dog in the backyard. That's not me, but that's the voice I use. The same is true if I'm writing for a children's publication. I use a different voice."

Problems with Her Publisher

After several years of freelancing, including doing articles for women's magazines, science journals, children's publications, and tons of articles for the horse industry, Bonnie decided to write a parents' guide to buying a first horse. "I naively thought that if I write it, they will buy it, and I will make billions."

Bonnie sold the manuscript to an East Coast publisher for no advance. "I had no clue about publishing. I shopped the book to publishers on my own, and sold it in 1990. This is where the caviar and champagne dreams began, but four years later the publisher was still sitting on that book. We had gone through the editing process, even made it to galleys, when they told me they had changed direction. They didn't want to do the book anymore."

This left Bonnie with a problem. In anticipation of the release of her best selling book, she had contacted many of the horse magazines she wrote for and offered to swap columns for full page ad space. The magazines were thrilled, and many accepted her offer. Then she discover she would have no product to sell because the book wasn't going to happen.

"I think failure only comes when you make the decision that you blew it," Bonnie states bluntly. "You can still get a win, though it may not be the win you had in mind. In my case I decided that I had to come up with product to fill those ads."

Publishing Booklets

Bonnie decided to sell booklets. "I used excerpts from that first unpublished book, did general booklets filled with safety information from articles I had written, and also used old articles that I put into booklet form. I had five in total."

What happened next completely surprised Bonnie. "The booklets I was absolutely sure would sell by the truckload, I couldn't give them away. One of them was *How to Prevent Fire in Your Barn*. This thing was jam packed with information on how you can save yourself from a huge nightmare, but nobody wanted that booklet.

"The booklets that I literally threw into the ad because there was space left for two more, I couldn't keep those in stock. One was *How to Avoid Buying a Lemon* and the other was *Debugging Your Horse,* both of which are now books. It was an interesting way to test market. Stumble in the dark long enough and you hit a light switch."

The booklets themselves were very simple without any color. Bonnie produced them by going to the local copy shop, and sold them for $4-$7. "The booklets were little, last minute uh-ohs, inexpensive and easy to buy. The covers each had a basic illustration I got from a clip art package. They were plain little booklets, but with the best information. The ads were all text and no pictures."

Publishing a Book

In 1994 Bonnie decided to rewrite her first book, *The Parents' Guide to Buying Your First Horse*, and publish it herself. "I wanted to write it true to what I had in mind originally. At the core of the book the other publisher and I had had a difference of opinion. I wanted to be explicit; they wanted to be very vague.

"For example, I said in the book, 'If you want your inexperienced child to grow old enough to marry someday, don't buy her a young Arabian mount because they are hot-blooded and hot-headed, easily spooked animals with a long standing reputation for hospitalizing their owners.' What the publisher wanted to print instead was that quarter horses make a lovely choice for a beginning rider."

Despite her experience with the booklets, Bonnie didn't accurately gauge the market for her first book. "I printed 3,000 copies and still have 700 copies left today. The content was sound, but I believe the reason why it didn't sell is because the information was provided in a very matter-of-fact fashion. If I rewrote that book now it would sell because I understand that I would have to write it to be more entertaining, more engaging, more marketable. Solid information in a clear format is not enough.

"As a writer I have to come to the realization that my definition of good is not necessarily the public's definition. That's one of the hard lessons I've learned. As a businesswoman, it's more important to publish books that my customers are looking for rather than use my own personal preferences as a compass."

Hosting an AOL Live Chat

Bonnie wrote her second book in self-defense. "I had contacted somebody from the pet care forum with AOL suggesting we swap out columns for ad space in the forum. They wrote back asking if I would be interested in hosting a live one hour chat in exchange for some co-op marketing. I agreed to host a live chat every Thursday night on horses. I discovered early on that people were coming on every week asking the same questions. On a live chat it is impossible to supply the ten pages of information to really solve a problem. So I would tell them to e-mail me privately and I would send them an article I had written about it."

Within a month Bonnie realized she was sending out the same stuff over and over again. "For the sake of convenience I wanted to put it all in a book, the top thirty problems people have with their horses. I would include two or three letters I had received about a problem during the years I was writing my syndicated horse column, say bucking, give my answers, and then add update letters I had received later from the writers.

"Clearly there was a need in the market for this book, and out of sheer laziness I was going to fill that need because it would be easier for me to send a chapter at a time to these people instead of cutting and pasting all these articles. I got release forms from everybody whose letters I used, cranked out the book, and I can't keep that thing on the shelf."

While deciding on the price for *Debugging Your Horse*, Bonnie asked her tack shop distributor for advice. "*Debugging* was 320 pages, line drawings only, paperback, no color art other than the cover. They said to keep the price under $20 and you'll sell volume. But *The Parents' Guide* was $16.95 for 150 pages. How was I going to justify charging only $2-$3 more for a book that was twice the size? I thought, I'm not doing charity work, so I'm asking $23.95."

Since her first book was selling so slowly, Bonnie printed only 1,000 copies of her second book instead of a matching first print run of 3,000. "We sold that printing in three to four months. Since my first book hadn't moved well, I was convinced this was a fluke, so I didn't want to order a reprint."

Bonnie did print another 1,000 copies and they sold, too. "I've reprinted that book three times now, 1,000 at a shot, and I'm about to go back again. The highest selling non-fiction horse book I am aware of sold 5,000 copies, so in this niche *Debugging Your Horse* is considered a primo book."

Branching Out

Wanting to break out of the limited market for horse books, Bonnie decided in 1997 to do a crossover book, *The Animal Lover's Guide to the Internet*, which included horses as well as dogs and cats, plus numerous other animals. "I was really focused on the web sites and the content of the book. As we got closer to the actual print date and talking about printing bids, one of the printers brought up the binding. I decided to do wire-o binding because it was a computer book and I wanted it to lie flat on a desk. What I didn't know at the time was that I needed a spine over the top of the wire-o for the bookstores. I made a boo-boo which has limited the book's marketability."

This mistake cost her sales, and to add insult to injury, the wire-o binding was more expensive than perfect binding. Bonnie says she blundered because she didn't think carefully about what it would mean to use a different binding. "No matter how close you are to the publishing date, every detail counts," Bonnie warns. "It's not acceptable to say, well, I got 99% of it right. Even after doing a couple of books, if there's any new thing in the equation, you are at the beginning of the learning curve again. You are responsible for going back out there and finding out information and getting up to speed again."

Bonnie took a middle-of-the-road position when deciding on her print run for this book, settling on 1,500 copies. She sold approximately 1,000 copies in the first year, but thinks she could have done better. "That book was supposed to be our cross-over book into bookstores and pet shops nationwide, and instead it is being marketed through associations, direct magazine ads, libraries and other avenues. That's not what we had planned."

Exploring Videos

"I had done TV stuff when we were in Oregon so I was very comfortable with the concept of producing something. The logical next product line was video," Bonnie says. But when she called her distributor to ask what average number of sales they had per video title, they said they sold only one hundred copies per year.

Bonnie decided to go ahead with her plans anyway because she could produce the videos for almost no cost. "Because my husband was doing volunteer work for the sheriff's department , we could use their fully outfitted studio, and I found a video house that needed help writing copy and press releases." Bonnie did another swap, her time and skills for their production time.

They produced two videos, *Debugging Techniques Part One* as a tie-in product for her best selling book, and a tape called *Trail Riding Rules of the Road*. The film was shot at a 14,000 acre horse ranch in California, and Bonnie did a promotional piece for the ranch in exchange for using it as the film location. "There were about twelve or fifteen people in the videos, and I gave them all copies. Our total production cost was about $100.

"We did the debugging video in 1997 and the other one in 1998. The return rate and the sales rate have been what we were told they would be."

Bonnie also learned firsthand about the rampant piracy of tapes. "I called video production houses across the country to ask if they were experiencing the same thing, and they laughed. We have discovered the necessity for shrink wrap and tapes that are fully refundable until and unless they are opened. That way they can't copy it and then send it back for a refund."

Despite what had looked like a profitable margin, Bonnie hasn't made a lot of money with the videos. "Our cost per unit is $3. The debugging tape goes for $34.95 and the trail video for $29.95. We produced them for near to nothing, but everyone was right. The video thing is not a very productive product line."

Deciding Against Publishing Other Authors

"I almost published a pharmaceutical book a couple of years ago," Bonnie says. She thought the pharmacist was knowledgeable plus very good-looking, an attribute she believes can make an author more marketable. Despite her interest in the book and her belief in the author, Bonnie decided against taking on the project.

"This guy knew as little about publishing as I did when I started. I was going to have to completely babysit the process just like any publisher, and I thought if I have to do that, it might as well be for one of my books. Otherwise I was going to have to stop writing books because there wouldn't be any creative juice left for months while I held his hand through the writing process and the editing process, the whole shooting match."

In the end Bonnie decided that she's not interested in publishing other authors. She isn't personally willing to invest the time, and she can't take on employees. "It's pointless to hire someone because I never know where we're going to be living next. By the time I trained them I'd be moving again."

The Covers

For her first book cover Bonnie used a photograph her husband had taken for a magazine article she had done. "We had a lot of still photos, and there was one particularly nice one of a white pony with a little girl standing next to him with all the right equipment, the helmet and the boots and all that. The girl was the daughter of the lady who owned the farm where we did the shoot. The woman was thrilled to have her daughter on the cover of our book. The irony was that the girl was a very generic looking twelve or thirteen year-old child, so many people thought it was a picture of a little boy."

For the cover of *Debugging Your Horse: A user-friendly guide to restoring your normally quiet horse after his hard disk has crashed!*, Bonnie hired a woman out of Arizona whose work she had admired in magazines. The style was cartoonish and featured a horse sitting at a computer. "The total cost of the cover was under $500 for the whole thing completely finished, ready to go to the printer, and I get comments from people all the time about that cover; they think it's hysterical."

Bonnie hired an artist named Bonnie Shields to do the artwork for the *Animal Lover's Guide* cover. "I had seen her work on a greeting card and fell in love with it. Most of her work is actually humorous greeting cards and t-shirts, that kind of thing. I tracked her down and we negotiated a deal."

Distributors and Catalogs

Bonnie sells her books directly as well as through distributors and via catalogs. "State Line Tack is probably the second largest catalog house in the country for the horse industry, and Libertyville Saddle Shop also carries our books in their catalog. For a long time I wasn't interested in getting into bed with Ingram and Baker & Taylor." Instead Bonnie sold her books through Western International, a company out of Nevada that sells books and videos to tack shops.

"The only reason we expanded our list of distributors in 1996 was because someone on the old PMA list serv said a publisher's obligation is to idiot proof the book buying process. That means putting your books every place a reader will potentially stumble across them."

When Bonnie first approached Baker & Taylor to pursue distribution through them, they told her it would cost $125 to be listed in their database. "I thought, are you nuts? So we passed and then four months later they contacted us and said they had standing orders — would we be willing to be included for free in their database?" This time the price was right, so Bonnie said yes.

K & B Products currently works with Unique and Bookazine as well as the two book wholesaler giants. "The good thing about Ingram and Baker & Taylor is our sales pattern. We've enjoyed a consistent three to four orders a week for five to fifteen books at a go, and no returns."

Fulfillment

Until 1999, Bonnie filled direct orders herself. "Because my husband and I travel all the time, I secured a 24-hour-a-day live answering service that took the orders and fielded the phone calls that were not order related," Bonnie explains. "Wherever I was they would fax my stuff to me at 6:00 p.m. my time. I would fill direct orders, and if it was a customer question I would handle that. Hiring them was probably one of the best investments I ever made. It cost $70 a month flat rate. The only additional charge was the cost to fax to me, and that was nominal. My total cost was about $83 a month."

Pleased as she was with her ability to offer a live human voice to her customers seven days a week, twenty-four hours a day at an affordable price, Bonnie eventually decided to do something different. "It was becoming very expensive to move all the books. When my husband recently accepted a job in Texas we brought a limited number of cases for each of the books. I left the rest stored in California and arranged to have them shipped here as I needed them to fill orders."

Next, Bonnie hired a full service book fulfillment company to handle taking phone calls and shipping orders for her. "I went with Book Clearing House. They charge me 30% for any order where they handle the complete fulfillment. This means that they answer the call and take the order, process the credit card, then pack and ship the product. For limited fulfillment where I receive the initial order, do the billing, and then fax the order to BCH for shipping only, they charge me 10%."

The main benefit that came with hiring BCH has been Bonnie's new sense of freedom. "I'm no longer tied to a phone," she rejoices. If she has the time, she still does her own fulfillment, but otherwise she lets BCH take over the responsibility. "When my schedule gets busy, it is a real treat and cheap at the price to have someone else handle the phones, take the orders, and ship the books."

Maximizing Speaking Engagements

"I speak at events because I want to get the pre-press publicity for my books," Bonnie says candidly. "For me the juice is what happens the three to four months before the events. I suck the life out of every pre-event press opportunity I can get, and the events themselves are sort of an afterthought."

Though Bonnie prefers to book an engagement months in advance so she has plenty of time to arrange pre-press, she manages to squeeze out as many leads as she can even with short-notice arrangements. "I did a large speaking engagement in San Diego for my niche market, the horse business. I had low expectations for the event because the organizers waited to finalize their roster of speakers. No one knew I was going to be at the event until thirty days out."

Bonnie figured she would focus on a breakfast meeting she had pre-arranged with another group of event organizers who wanted to see her in action before booking her for their event the following year. However, while she was in town she made a number of important connections.

"Not only did I meet the organizers of the other event and secure the deal, I also met a large animal vet who was new at the speaking thing. She wanted to hang out with me for the weekend.

We had a great time and agreed to work together on co-op projects in the future."

Shortly after Bonnie returned home, she received a call from the vet. "She writes a column for a major vet magazine and had just received a letter from a vet who was looking for a book he could recommend to his clients about buying a first horse." Bonnie's title, *A Parent's Guide to Buying That First Horse*, ended up getting a mention in a magazine targeted to a key segment of her market. The vet included Bonnie's 1-800 number and web site address in the article.

"The beauty of this incident was that I had never considered marketing this particular books to veterinarians until I met this vet," Bonnie says. "During our conversation on the phone she mentioned how often people asked her for tips on buying a horse. She liked our book and wanted to share it with other vets around the country so they, too, could refer their clients to it."

In addition, Bonnie learned more about her value as a speaker. "I was told about some of the 'deals' other big speakers were asking for and getting! It was a huge eye-opening experience for me." She also met a Canadian speaker who was interested in doing some co-op activities to promote their books together. Plus the event gave Bonnie the excuse to send out 400 press releases about her appearance to magazines around North America.

"While selling books is a primary goal at a speaking engagement, the list of benefits goes way beyond that," Bonnie says. "If you keep your eyes wide open and look for opportunities before, during, and after the event, you can maximize your profitability with every speaking engagement you do."

Advice to New Publishers

"I think what stops most people from pursuing self-publishing is the illusion that it's unattainable," Bonnie says, "but even if you don't know squat about what you're doing, you can move forward. You must be willing to look like an idiot. And you must make plans with your business and realize that before the ink is dry your plans will change. You have to be flexible enough to have plans A, B, and C.

"Everything you do has to be coming from the place of the end customer. The reader is not interested in your view unless it will help them. If you are clear about who you are writing for, the message you are trying to share, and what packaging your readers want, you are filling a niche. You are producing product that fulfills a need."

Bonnie thinks self-publishing can be a great business if someone is willing to do the research, then follow it up with lots of promotion. "How well do you understand your market and your demographics, and how effective are you as a salesman? The good news and the bad news is the same: the opportunities to sell are limitless, but if you have access to every market in the country, so does the competition.

"You need to be consistently marketing. I still do the free ads, all of them in exchange for two syndicated articles a month for these regional horse magazines. That's between fifteen and thirty ads per month, and they run between a quarter page and a half page in size."

Bonnie focuses on her daily goals. "My day isn't finished until I've done at least two new marketing things to promote my products. I'm in my office by 5:30 a.m. because I've discovered I can get almost eight hours of work done between then and 9:00 a.m. I am alone in the office. There are no phones ringing and no distractions."

To make sure she hits the ground running, she writes down her goals for the following day before she leaves her office. "I maintain a journal as a functional, practical means to outline what I expect to accomplish the next day. The journal entry for tomorrow is filled out by 4:00 p.m. the day before. This allows me to have a plan of attack for the next morning."

Keeping a positive frame of mind has also helped Bonnie to do well. "Remember that it will be hard to succeed if you surround yourself with people talking doom and gloom all of the time. Be careful to take in a steady stream of positive stuff."

Chapter Ten

Daring to Publish Mysteries

The modern non-fiction path to self-publishing success has been well blazed by hundreds of writers, but self-publishers of fiction are still pioneers. Connie Shelton was one of the few fiction writers to start a well-known small publishing house in the 1990s. By the spring of 1999 she had grown her mystery imprint to a total of twenty-seven titles by eight different authors.

Connie had originally tried to get her manuscripts published the traditional way. "I had written a couple of books that were mainstream novels and sent them around quite a bit. I kept getting these flattering rejection letters. 'We like the characters, we like the setting,' one thing or another, then there was always a BUT, always some reason they couldn't take it."

While she was waiting for someone to say yes, Connie began to hang around other authors and to attend conferences. As she talked with authors and discovered what they went through with their New York publishers, she began to think she didn't really want to go that route at all.

"I had begun to write a mystery series, and I decided to start my own company and see what I could do. I wrote three books in the series before I began the company in 1994, and that gave me some material to start with. I printed one title thinking, 'I'll see how this goes, and if it totally bombs, I won't do another one.' It went really well. I reached the break even point within ninety days, around 1,000 books sold from an initial print run of 3,000 copies. So I went ahead and did the second book about six or eight months later, and then I did the third one a year after the second one."

She hired Marilyn and Tom Ross, owners of About Books, Inc., to help her develop a marketing campaign. "I followed the Ross' suggestions that I get advance review copies out very early and that kind of thing. I was very fortunate to get a review in *Booklist* which really did help library sales. That's an advantage to doing fiction in hardcover, it gives you access to the library market."

Connie didn't restrict herself to the standard list of review sources. "There are a lot of fan magazines and that kind of thing out there that review new books. I began to accumulate a pretty good list of reviewers of my own aside from the so-called main stream media sources. By getting away from the generic biggies like *The New York Times* and *The Los Angeles Times*, I found a lot of mystery publications that really reach out to the fans of the genre. That helped, getting into that inner circle of mystery fans."

In the meanwhile, Connie began to get very involved in the mystery community. She went to conferences and met a lot of the mystery booksellers. "At about the same time my first book came out, I attended my first mystery conference. Probably one of my biggest fears before publishing was wondering who was going to buy a book from somebody they had never heard of. I think all of us as readers can identify with that uncertainty about whether you want to buy a book when you have never heard anything about it or the author. But I found that mystery booksellers were open to new authors."

The Onslaught of Hopeful Writers

Connie didn't originally plan to publish other authors, but writers soon began to approach her. "People would buy a book and see the name Intrigue Press. They'd go, 'This must be a new publisher.' They would look on the copyright page to get the address, and the next thing I knew I was getting manuscripts whether I advertised for them or not."

Word of mouth inside the genre also brought her press to the attention of hopeful authors. "I get calls at least a couple times a week where they say, 'I was talking to so-and-so at the murder bookstore in whatever town, and they say you publish books like the one I have just written.'"

Currently, Connie is working with seven other authors in addition to publishing her own work. "Several of our authors are writing series, so that pretty much commits us to a certain number of new books. Most of the authors are producing a book a year. We have a really good working relationship with all of them so if they say, 'Are you ready for the next one?' I say yes. They don't feel like they have to shop their manuscript around and send it to a lot of places to get it sold, and I feel like we have the next book in the series all locked up and ready to go."

Connie met her seven authors in a variety of ways. "Most have come to me through referrals or because I knew them personally. Only one came over the transom. She was the second author I took on. From time to time I get recommendations from somebody who says. "So-and-so is a really good author. I know she's looking for a publisher for her next book; do you want to take a look at it?'"

On occasion some of her authors already had a major publisher taking their new titles, but backlist titles were being allowed to go out of print. "In a couple of cases I've picked up older titles that have been previously published by someone else, but the authors got their rights back.

"Once I was approached by an author's agent and in another case I knew the author. We would e-mail back and forth on various topics, and one day he was feeling kind of down because three of his previous books were going out of print. They were becoming difficult to find. This author is still with St. Martin Press and had a new hardcover coming out, but they weren't interested in taking his three older books to paperback."

Connie was interested in reissuing these books because she understands how mystery readers approach their reading. The first book she wrote and published, *Deadly Gamble*, is her strongest backlist book. "We sell more copies of that book because mystery readers like to read a series in the order it was written. If they first learn about me at book number four, they want to go back and read the series from the start. I think you would find this is true in all fiction genres."

Intrigue Press published the author's third book in paperback in the spring of 1999 to coincide with the release of his new hardcover. "We plan to do the two older books this coming fall or next spring because I understand that the existing stock is gone, and people are having a real hard time finding those books."

Limitations of Time and Money

Connie used to read every submission she received, and she would send the author a little note offering comments or suggestions. "It finally dawned on me that I do not have the time for that anymore. I have a continual marketing job on my hands for the books I already have."

Trying to find the time to do her own writing has become difficult. In addition to her backlist, she publishes around eight books each year consisting of four or five new hardcovers as well as the paperback reprints from the previous year. Plus she faces financial limits.

"You discover when you get into this business that publishing really has very poor cash flow. In most cases you have to have the books printed before you can collect a dime on any of them. There are certain cases where you can pre-sell a large quantity and that helps pay for your print run, but within the trade you pretty much wait months for your money. Ingram pays in ninety days, so if you pay for your print run on January 1st and the books start to sell then, it may be April 1st before you get paid for any of them. So cash flow is always a problem."

To free up money to print more new titles would mean letting other titles go out of print, something Connie is loath to do. She thinks it is crucial to keep all of the books of a series in print. "I know how mystery readers think. I've gotten to be friends with many of the mystery booksellers, and they tell me it is so frustrating to them when they see a customer walking in the door who would buy every book by an author, but they won't want to read the later books until they read the earlier ones.

"In most cases if an author has a mystery series it contains a continuing character that goes from one book to the next. I think that's why readers enjoy going back and reading books in sequence because they like to see how that character evolves, how they started out, and how their personal lives change along with how they solve the mysteries. To avoid having to search for a rare, out-of-print book, a bookseller may recommend a different author or series to a reader."

Connie is looking at a couple of options to keep her titles in print. "I could reprint the same as always and have another big ol' pile of books sitting here as they gradually sell, or I could do the print-on-demand kind of thing. I'm trying to figure out if it would make more sense to print a couple of hundred books that might last us for two to three months, or to go ahead and do a larger print run."

Evaluating New Authors

"The marketing push it takes to launch a brand new author is quite a bit more time consuming than bringing out the fourth book of an author who already has a following," Connie explains. "If I have an author who I know will be out there self-promoting, that's definitely going to weigh in their favor because the publisher can't do it all. I think even the New York houses have this attitude, they just don't tell their authors. I tell my authors up front. You are going to do most of the promotion for your book. You will have to line up your own book tours and pay your own way to the conferences.

"We will co-op some of the expense with them on postcards, print ads, or promotional giveaways. For example, maybe we'll pay for the postcards and they'll pay for the postage to mail them out or vice versa. We'll do that together, but I don't lead them to believe there is a publicist here at the publishing house. Like once you hand over your manuscript, you are done. That doesn't happen here. I have an assistant who does everything from the editing and proof reading down to the mundane tasks of sticking labels on mailings, but she is part-time."

Connie believes in doing book signings if they are done economically. "Sometimes you have a good crowd and maybe the very next day you have no one show up. I encourage our authors to devise a tour within a comfortable distance from their home. They can do a couple of book signings in a weekend by doing a quick drive out of town. I don't encourage them to spend money on plane tickets and hotels all over the country. At least at our level, we don't have nationally known authors and that kind of thing wouldn't pay off for them."

Connie encourages her authors to attend conferences that draw lots of mystery fans. "The big one, Bouchercon, is in October with 2,500 fans. Most of the mystery conferences are set up with panels and if someone registers as an author, the organizers will do their best to schedule that person for a panel. The authors get a chance to talk about their books, the process of writing, whatever the theme is. It gives the audience a chance to associate an author with a book. Later the authors go to the autographing area and sign books.

"We also tell our authors not to spend lots of money on traveling because it's hard to earn it back. They could end up spending most of their advance doing promotion. But from what I hear, authors published by the big houses do the same thing."

Receiving Submissions

"We used to be listed in the *Novel and Short Story Writers Market*, and I couldn't even begin to wade through the submissions. I was having to tell everybody NO. It was discouraging for them and it took a lot of our time. I took out our listing this year. Pretty much every time someone contacts me and says, 'We are compiling a list of publishers who are interested in submissions, do you want to be on the list?' I tell them no. We are too small."

The quality of the submissions Connie receives varies wildly. "I would say probably 20% could no how, no way, be published, 20% could be made publishable with minor editing and a little encouragement, and the biggest percentage that's in the middle could be published, but would take way more editing, hand holding and help than what I would have the time to do. I think that is pretty true with most publishers.

"We receive about ten submissions each week. Publishers like Berkley and HarperCollins must get hundreds. An editor can afford to be very, very picky. It behooves a writer to make sure that their work is as nearly perfect as they can get it before they ever send it out. There are just thousands of submissions hitting publishing houses all the time."

A lot of the submissions she receives aren't appropriate for Intrigue. Assuming that they are mysteries, their lengths still may not work. "I get everything. People say, 'I've written a new mystery novel, it is 40,000 words,' and I say, 'No, dear, that is a novella.' On the other hand some submissions are 140,000 words.

"I have a form letter of guidelines. I usually look at things between 75,000 to 90,000 words, not significantly above or below that range. Also, though I swore I would never do this, I have a form rejection letter. Basically it states that we have as much inventory as we can use for the next couple of years. It's the truth. I have received a couple of submissions that made the hair on my neck stand up they were so good, but I didn't have a publishing slot at the time.

"It's really unfair to tie someone up with a contract when you know it's going to be two years before you can print the book. That's the way I see it. I like to leave them free to keep looking because I know what it's like to be a writer. You feel that time is just pressing in on you and you want that book in your hands; you can taste it. The form letter says good luck finding another publisher."

Occasionally Connie will recommend that an author try the self-publishing route. "It depends on whether or not they seem like a person who could successfully publish on their own. A lot of people, writers especially, their interests lie in being creative and artistic. They really have no business experience."

Making Room for New Authors

Connie does find a spot for a new author occasionally depending on the circumstances. Though she usually wants to publish multiple titles from any author, she'll make exceptions for people like Linda Grant. "She is still being published by Scribner in hardcover, and she is a dynamite promoter. She is the past president of Sisters in Crime and is very well known in the mystery field. We republished her first book. I didn't know what to expect. It had been out of print for quite a while, like close to ten years, but knowing how mystery readers think, I knew we would do okay. Actually it has turned out to be one of our best selling paperbacks."

Connie also tries to provide some variety in her list. Because she personally likes to read the more light-hearted mysteries, the Charlie Parker mysteries she writes are on the lighter side. "The Sophie Dunbar series is light-hearted and humorous, and the Steve Brewer series is very humorous, but Alex Matthews' books are completely different. She deals with some very gritty subjects, child abuse and Satanism and HIV, and drugs and prostitution. She doesn't get into a lot of blood and gut descriptions, but the subject matter is pretty intense. Linda Grant's main character is a kind of hard-boiled female investigator. She does martial arts and is not above kicking bad guys in the face. She doesn't come across as too tough to be true, but she is definitely no wuss. So we do have variety in that sense.

"A book I'm looking at is a historical mystery an agent wants me to read. Historical mysteries are very popular right now, so it might be a nice addition to the list. But it's a brand new author, a first novel. Usually I am doing good if I can introduce one new first novel every couple of years, and we have a first novel coming out this fall. The historical novel, if I take it, would come out the fall of 2000 or maybe the spring of 2001."

Her other new novelist, Susan Slater, is writing a series set on an Indian pueblo. "It's kind of reminiscent of Tony Hillerman's characters and type of work. I think she'll do well. I foresee a bright future there."

Contract Terms

Intrigue offers an advance of $500. "I realize that is pitifully low, and I always feel like I am apologizing for that, but I think most of the authors see the wisdom when I explain that we have X amount of dollars that we can devote to any one book. I would rather give them a smaller advance and have the difference go to promotion and publicity. If the book sells, they'll get their money anyway.

"Royalties are 10% on the net sales price. Sometimes that is on the first 2,000 copies and then it escalates slightly. I have a standard contract and most of the authors who come direct to me sign it. But the authors who come with an agent manage to tweek little things here and there. Even though the agents say it is a very author friendly contract, they want to change at least one thing. I guess they feel they haven't earned their money unless they do that.

"I used to worry that agents would try to insist on something like a $10,000 advance, and I just don't have the cash to do that. But I've found that most of them are realistic, especially when they represent new and midlist authors. Most have been fairly easy to work with."

Developing and Retaining Authors

The sales numbers for Connie's authors increase with each successive book in their series. "You know, it just takes a while. Big publishers used to hang in there with their authors, knowing that sales would be so-so in the beginning. After an author had a decent backlist built up then they would do the 'break out' book.

"One of my big hopes as a publisher is that a book will come across my desk with that type of potential, and I am smart enough to recognize it. Then I hope I have the money, the time, and the resources to do something with it. That's the next step for Intrigue because four of our authors have four to five books in their series out there, and I'm thinking that by the time these people have eight or ten books published we should be thinking about breaking them out."

Switching up to this different level of marketing concerns Connie. "What will that entail? How expensive will it be and will I have the guts to do it? Will I have the cash to not only pay for the printing but to pay for the advertising or whatever we need to do?"

Though Connie intends to stick with her authors, she realizes that some of them may decide to find a new publisher at some point in the future. "Some of my authors are with me out of personal loyalty. Others, if the right offer came along, would leave me in a heart beat. In that case, may they become famous. I would still have the rights to their backlist."

This attitude is one of the reasons Connie acquired the rights to Linda Grant's first book. "My main thought was to look to the future because her hardcover publisher is talking about breaking her out at some point. Then one of two things will happen. Either we can issue a new edition of this older book and sell bunches of them, or if her publisher wants to do that, then we're holding some very lucrative rights. One way or another I'll win as long as she keeps writing and they keep promoting her. At least that's my theory."

Print Runs and Binding Choices

"We pretty much do everything hardcover first and then paperback. We time the paperback version to come out when the author's next hardcover is released. We've found that aside from the libraries and the collectors, and there are a lot of collectors who prefer hardcovers, there is a limited market for the hardcover version. You need to price the book so people can afford it in the mass markets."

The hardcover mysteries are generally priced at $22.95 while the mass market paperbacks are in the $5.50-$5.95 range. Intrigue Press has also taken over a collection of short stories called *Murder by 13* written by members of the Los Angeles chapter of Sisters in Crime. Published in trade paperback size, it's priced at $10.95.

Connie orders relatively large print runs for a small press. "Hardcover print runs are usually 2,000-3,000 copies, and we usually do 5,000-7,500 copies for the mass market paperbacks."

Getting a Distributor for Fiction

"I tried and tried to get a distributor to talk to me when I had a couple of books out, and they all kind of hemmed and hawed, and said fiction is a tough sell. At the time it was a big disappointment not to get a distributor."

About two years later, when Connie had seven or eight books in print, a distributor, Midpoint Trade Books, approached her. "It all fell into place. I can see from the distributor's point of view why they don't want to represent every one and two-book publisher because many of those books have a defined period of time they are out there, maybe a year or two, and then they're gone."

One of the reasons Connie decided to sign a semi-exclusive agreement with Midpoint was because they represented Write Way Publishing. "It's another mystery press and I figured if their reps are going in to the mystery buyer at Barnes & Noble, it's going to look a lot better if they have plenty of mysteries to present. So far our relationship has worked out really well. They handle a big portion of the fulfillment. They handle all of the major wholesalers like Ingram and Baker & Taylor, and they send their reps out to the chains."

Midpoint also handles some of the larger independent bookstore accounts such as the Tattered Cover in Denver, Colorado, but they don't handle the small specialty stores. "They left us free to work with our mystery bookstores. Basically any independent bookstore that wants to order direct from us can do so. This is helpful when we have a book signing coming up, and the bookstore waits to order books less than a week ahead. If they went through the whole channel, the wholesaler and the distributor, they wouldn't get them in time. We can usually offer same-day fulfillment if they are in a rush."

Marketing

Connie has continued to get reviews for almost all of her books from at least one of the major pre-publication review magazines. "Everything we have published in hardcover has been reviewed in either *Publishers Weekly*, *Library Journal* or *Booklist*. One of our spring 1999 books got reviews in all three."

Though it's impossible to track orders directly to a review, Connie does believe reviews translate into sales. "When I visit with booksellers and librarians, they tell me that they order every book they see reviewed in any of those three publications. It's not even based on what the review said. They figure if it got reviewed, that's enough for them to purchase it.

"I operate on the throw-the-mud-at-the-wall theory. I am very generous with review copies and I send out at least a couple of hundred books. When we get new titles in, I send out a blanket e-mail to my reviewer list saying that if they will review the book then I will be happy to send a copy. Just let me know if you want one. I get a lot of positive response with people saying they'll review them."

Connie uses a free newsletter to keep in touch with her company's readers. "We get names for our mailing list at conferences, off our web site, and ask for them in all of our print advertising plus in the backs of our books. We have around 1,200 names. We send the newsletter through the mail, but if any person who signs up for the list cares to give me an e-mail address, then we send them a heads-up whenever we have new books out."

Connie's marketing plan is directed more to fans rather than to stores. "I figure the fans drive sales. If they go into a store and request a certain author, and enough people do that, then that store will order the books. But if you market to the stores, and they say, 'Okay, we'll give your book a chance,' they may order it, and no one ever comes in to buy it. Then those copies are going to come back to you."

Because of her approach, Connie's return rate is relatively low. "Generally it runs between 8-12%. I feel pretty fortunate about that because I hear about other people with 40-50% return rates. That's scary."

The biggest percentage of Connie's sales go through bookstores. "Our hardcovers do well in libraries. I would guess that 30% go to libraries, 50% to bookstores, and the remaining 20% are direct sales or over the Internet."

Intrigue Press has its own web site, though sales haven't been enough to allow the site to pay for itself. "I look at it more as a constantly running advertisement. I can send people to it at any time. It's a place that will last forever and can be easily updated. I think it's worth doing, but in general I wouldn't advise publishers that they can really make money with their web sites. The 20% discount we offer helps generate the sales we do get, but we charge $3.00 for shipping, so that basically offsets the discount. We sell far more books through Amazon.com, probably because they've become a brand name in the business. People trust ordering from them more than from a smaller site."

Connie's experience with Amazon.com has been positive. "We joined their Advantage program in 1998 and they have been selling books consistently. They don't sell more than all other booksellers combined, but more than any other one bookseller. I have mixed feeling about Amazon because I am basically pro independent bookstores and I don't like to see them suffer. In discussions with readers, I've learned that they still like to be in a store to feel and see and touch the books. But there are growing numbers who choose Internet ordering. We try to cater to both types."

The only book trade show she attends is BookExpo America (BEA). "I work out of my distributor's booth. They pay the cost of getting the booth and they will let any of their publishers come and stand there all day. I give away free paperback books or some giveaway like ball-point pens."

Connie attends three to six mystery conferences each year. "If I can't attend a conference I can at least get marketing materials there. If I'm not going personally, one of our authors will be. That's the beauty of publishing multiple authors. I send them a box of stuff to put out on the giveaway table. Extra newsletters are particularly good. I put a bright fluorescent sticker on them that says, 'For a free subscription call 1-800 or visit our web site.' We have also donated materials for the registration packets for several of the mystery conferences. We've given paperback books several times or an imprinted item. We try to have a presence of some kind at every conference."

The newsletter has inspired some people to send Connie strange mail. "I got this letter one time that initially infuriated me, but then I just had to laugh. This guy told us we were 'clueless'. He wasn't interested in buying anything from us, he wanted us to publish his book. He would, though, be happy to stay in contact with us if an advance and contract would be forthcoming." Connie sent the gentleman a letter advising him that in query letters he shouldn't call the editor clueless nor admit that he doesn't read the publisher's other books. "I was happy to take his name off our list."

Exploring Non-Fiction

When Connie started Intrigue Press, she only planned to publish mysteries. When she decided to do her first non-fiction book, she realized she needed a more generic name. "I incorporated under the name Columbine Publishing Group, Inc., and made Intrigue Press into an imprint." Since then she has published a total of three non-fiction books, each in a completely different area.

"I wrote *Publish Your Own Novel* because people kept asking me how to market fiction. Plus I was getting invited to speak at conferences a lot. One of the things you find when you go somewhere as a speaker is it's fine to have your one hour in the limelight, but if you don't have a book to sell at the back of the room, it hasn't paid off for you in any way. You are just giving away your time."

Publish Your Own Novel was picked up by the Writers Digest Book Club. "The copies they bought paid for the entire print run so I wasn't under pressure to sell enough copies through back-of-the-room sales to pay for the printing. We printed 3,000 copies and they took 1,000."

Connie hasn't made a huge push to sell this title, partly because she's been so busy with all her other books. "For a while I ran little classified ads in writers' magazines offering a free report on why it was hard to get published. Of course the report was designed to tell them that an alternative would be to publish their manuscript themselves. The ads sold the book consistently as long as I kept running them."

The book has also sold well at conferences where Connie is a speaker, and has been adopted by other speakers as a course reference when they do presentations on publishing. "It's received great reviews by many who have gone the self-publishing route in fiction. With all the new developments in Internet marketing and print-on-demand innovations, I've been considering doing an updated version."

Connie published her second non-fiction book as a favor to her community. "I was the president of the writers' group in my little town of Angel Fire when we were approached by our chamber of commerce. They said they had people in their office all the time who wanted a book on the history of the area. So the writers' group took on the project of writing the history of the Moreno Valley."

Connie did the layout for the book on a volunteer basis and also coordinated the printing job. "We are the publisher of record, but really the writers' group and the chamber of commerce are doing all of the distribution."

The third book came about because Connie met a writer at a conference. "She showed me this book called *Sign Here: How to Understand Any Contract Before You Sign*. It had been published by one of the biggies several years before. They had done real well with it and had let it go out of print."

Connie thought it might continue to do well for her. "We brought that one out in February of 1998. We put the author in a series of interview shows. I had hoped it would take off like gang busters and sell a gillion copies, but it hasn't done that well. It paid for itself and made a little profit, that's all."

Though Connie would possibly look at another non-fiction book, she intends to primarily concentrate on mysteries. "I learned this from doing the legal book. I could have given that book a whole lot more attention if I weren't in the mystery field. It's so much easier for me to market the mysteries because that's what I'm doing anyway. Adding another mystery doesn't send us off in another direction. If I were to add a romance book it would also be a whole different thing. I feel we have found our niche, mysteries, and ought to stick with it."

Covers

Connie pays between $600-$2,000 for a cover. "We have had a couple of covers that were losers. Though I know what it feels like to be an author, and I like to let authors have some input, one thing I've learned is not to let the author push me around. Thinking from a strictly marketing standpoint, the author's ideas are not always good.

"One story was about a client who comes in for therapy and it comes out that he was abused as a child. This terrible secret has hung over the family for years, so the author thought that having a cute, innocent, little boy sitting on the floor with a dark shadow hanging over him would be illustrative of the story. She's right, it is, but too many people thought it was a kid-in-jeopardy book, that there would be a lot of description of a child being hurt or abused. It turned some buyers away.

"For the second story the author had found an older book on her shelf with a cover of a windswept scene, a woman wearing a wind-whipped cape, a kind of gothic looking picture with a dark figure running away in the background. We tried something similar, but it looked like a slasher book. The title of the book, *Satan's Silence*, didn't help. Looking at the book's cover you got the idea it was something satanic and really gory, and it isn't except for one scene where the therapist confronts the Satanists during a ritual. We had a number of booksellers say they probably could have sold the book except that the cover was awful."

The covers for both these books were redone when they went to paperback. "I probably could have prevented having to redo them if I had gone back to the basics originally and taken the covers to a store and looked at all the other mysteries lined up. I could have seen that these covers just didn't fit in with what every other mystery looks like."

Other covers Connie was unsure about, however, did well. "The artist had read some books by one of our authors, and she came up with almost cartoonish covers. I thought they would be a turn-off, but they've done really well. Maybe when people are dealing with murder and mayhem making the cover a little humorous is a good thing."

Instead of relying only on her own judgement, Connie has learned to ask her distributor for help. "I will send Midpoint color copies of the concept for the cover art and ask them what they think. They have given me some good feedback. I have had a little doubt about a cover and they've said it's great, don't touch it, and other ones, well, you should do this and that. We do it because they are out there talking to the booksellers and working with the chains. It makes a difference because if they feel that a cover is bad, they are going to have a harder time selling that book."

Advice

Connie believes that a press should specialize in a given area. "Pick a niche and stay with it. It is so much easier to do your marketing once you get a few books that will appeal to the same readers. With all of your marketing materials, catalogs, mailings, and brochures, you can market five books just as easily as you can market one because you are sending the information out to the same group of people. They get to know your books and your press begins to get a reputation. That's all important; building a business identity.

"For example, I was at a mystery conference in Albuquerque in 1999. When I walked into the hotel a guy I knew greeted me and said, 'People are talking about you. They are saying really good things. They are impressed with the kinds of books Intrigue Press is publishing and the way you treat your authors.' That made me feel great, but it goes back to building an identity and finding a niche.

"Otherwise what happens if you do one mystery title and then a sci-fi title, then a mainstream novel and a couple of romances? You are never going to get really well known in a niche." Connie also recommends not calling your books mainstream novels. "It's too general. In terms of marketing to the public and to bookstores, you need to be able to define your novels in some sort of a niche category."

For larger publishers, Connie recommends reading *Publishing for Profit* by Thomas Woll. "Once you have four or five titles in print, it's a really good book as far as telling you how to set up spread sheets to chart your cash flow, handle pricing, just how to conduct your publishing program. It's a step beyond most publishing books that give you a lot of the success stories and how great it can be. It covers what to do now that you are publishing full-time and have a garage stacked with books."

Connie cautions that it can take awhile to generate spendable profits. Starting a publishing company is like opening any new business. "I think you are doing well if you break even in the first two to three years. I haven't been surprised that I haven't made any vast profits at the five-year mark. Expect success to come slowly. Take the time to build your list and your authors and your following. And keep some first edition copies of each of your authors' books; they could become valuable. You never know who's going to hit it big."

Postscript

Shortly after this interview, Connie received an offer for her mystery imprint, Intrigue Press. "The decision to sell Intrigue wasn't easy. It was my baby and hard to let go of, but the buyer came courting and made an offer that was hard to refuse. I can't name numbers, but it's a good start on retirement for me."

The opportunity to sell came at a crucial point in her development of Intrigue Press. "Intrigue was really at a crossroads. I either had to expand, move into a larger office, and hire more help, which I didn't really want to do, or sell to someone who had those resources." Her publishing work load was also making it difficult for Connie to squeeze in time to write her mysteries.

Connie's biggest concern was how a sale would affect her authors. "I knew they would be surprised, shocked, or upset, and I wanted to be sure they were taken care of."

The buyer agreed to keep the existing titles and authors, and plans to expand the list. "All in all, it's turned out very well. The money has been good and the freedom is nice."

Connie will stay busy with the two small businesses she co-owns with her husband as well as the bookstore she owns with a partner. And, of course, she'll be working on her next Charlie Parker mystery.

Chapter Eleven

Selling Directly to the Consumer

Former Canadian Gayle Mitchell sells most of her gambling books directly to consumers, but she rarely leaves her Arizona home to do it. "Most of my sales come from radio interviews. I've done over 600 shows so far. Generally I do twenty to thirty interviews a month.

"85% of the radio stations I've been on have me back. I'll call them and say, 'I was on three months ago, I'm the gambling lady, can we talk casino gambling again?' I have a program in my computer that reminds me to call these stations automatically every two months. Most of the time, however, the stations call me, and about 15 stations call every two to three months."

Before appearing on a particular show, Gayle has tried to predict how many books she'll sell by looking at the demographics for that city or station. "But you never know what type of results you'll get. You just have no idea. When Albuquerque called to set up an interview, I went, oh, well, nothing big, but wow! I sold over 40 books.

"For a Miami show I thought, whoa, look out, the phone will ring, but then nothing. You have to be up and energetic no matter what because you just don't know what could happen. I really like the call-in format because I get my best sales when I can answer questions."

Gayle originally tried to get on radio shows by contacting them directly. She signed up with a service to receive the names of shows and their producers plus their telephone and fax numbers. When the results disappointed her, she tried placing ads in *Radio/TV Interview Report*.

"They are the best. It saved me so much time. Rather than slogging away and spending time and money sending out faxes and calling producers, they called me," Gayle says. To take advantage of the multiple ad discount, she bought three ads at a time. "The report comes out three times a month, the 1st, 10th, and the 20th. I can choose which issue I want for an ad. I find I get the best results advertising in the last issue of each month."

Being the first widely recognized female expert in the world of casino gambling has helped Gayle get air time. "The media prefers to present 'firsts'. I had to work hard to break through the 'felt-covered' ceiling held by male gambling authors. In my books I write extensively about slots and video poker, and I know I was ridiculed by the male writers, especially when I wrote about slots. But now many of those same authors have produced books on both games."

Whenever Gayle is booked for a radio show, she sends a page of questions to the interviewer in advance. "It makes them sound smart. Only half of the time do they ask me to send them a book." She also sends freebie strategy cards or booklets as give-aways for the station. "Plus I send one strategy card marked 'for your receptionist' with my toll free number and the web site URL highlighted, and a personalized, signed, thank you note."

She also does her best to give each interview a local slant. "I try to mention local casinos that are good places to play. The very best place to play is Vegas, but sometimes the listeners can't go there." Her interviews last anywhere from five minutes to one hour. One exceptional interview, though, extended into 1 1/2 hours because the calls kept coming.

While on the air, Gayle mentions both her web site URL and her toll free number several times. "I notice the surge in sales after any radio interview. I now offer a free strategy card to any listener who calls, even if they don't buy. They get our four page flyer that goes out with the freebie card, and I get lots of additions to my mailing list."

Gayle included a worldwide casino travelogue in her second book, *More Casino Gambling Made Easier (More Winning Strategies, Casino Selections & Intelligent Gambling)*, with the idea that she could broaden her topic from gambling to travel as well. "But I've found out that Americans are not world travelers like Canadians are. When I started to sell the second book through the radio shows I got no response when I mentioned these other casinos. Now I barely mention them. Most of my interviews are taken up with strategies for the 75% of gamblers who play slots and video poker. I zero in on that."

Taking the Orders

"I give my 1-800 number out on the air. I have a separate line that goes into a voice box. I get very few hang-ups. Callers hear a recording that tells them about our latest special offers with bonuses, and instructs them to leave their ordering information: name, mailing address, and credit card number."

In case people are uncomfortable leaving that information on a machine, Gayle offers to fax or mail them an order form instead. "I tell them it's faster to use a credit card because their order will be out of our warehouse in 72 hours. More than 90% give their credit card numbers and over 85% will tell me where they heard about the book."

Gayle cautions other small publishers using the same system to keep their message simple. "I was offering different freebies as a bonus. If callers bought one set of books they would get one freebie, and if they bought two sets they got two different freebies. That was too confusing."

She handles the fulfillment herself. "A year or so ago my last child left home, so I use one bedroom as an office and another bedroom for storage. I sell each of my first two books, *Casino Gambling Made Easier: How a Rank Amateur Casino Gambler Can Learn to Win Using Intelligent Gambling* and *More Casino Gambling Made Easier*, individually for $17.95, or the two books as a set for $32.00. The shipping and handling are included for all our products because people are sick of paying extra. Plus I give them free strategy cards telling them what and where are the best slots, where Las Vegas locals play and win, and tips on video poker strategy."

Being on a publishers' list serv helped Gayle to reduce her shipping costs. "I was sending out these two books by priority mail for $3.20. Then I learned about sending books special rate." Since her books together weigh less than a pound, Gayle reduced her postage to $1.13.

Trying Audio Tapes

Before Gayle published her first book, she tried to sell other items, starting with multi-level marketing for newsletters. Then she joined a membership club of people selling books by mail order. She wanted to offer gambling items so she started to sell a newsletter and some books written by a gambling expert with 40 years experience.

Next she made some audio tapes about gambling. "It didn't really work out. It cost so much money and the sales were so slow that I nearly didn't get around to writing my first book." Eventually she sold all 400 tapes and was glad to be rid of them. "But I knew there was still a huge market out there for this information."

Prejudice Against Gambling Books

"I thought I would go through the big book distributors and sell my first book through the chains," says Gayle. "But Borders wouldn't talk to me and neither would Barnes & Noble. They won't carry my books in their stores, though they will sell them on the Internet. I'm in the Amazon Advantage program, and they produce the best sales online. My two single title books about slots and video poker, *Video Poker Made Easier (Winning Strategies for Serious Players)* and *All Slots Made Easier (Winning Strategies for Basic Slots, Progressives & Newest Versions)* have been rated first in their categories on Amazon.com.

"It took me the longest time to get a distributor. I kept mailing out books and following up." Unique finally agreed to take her first book. "I really like them. They send their checks out on time and I get the feeling they sell a lot to libraries. Libraries have finally jumped over this gambling prejudice thing."

Because of her troubles getting into the bookstores, Gayle decided to sell her book herself. "I'm selling 90% of my books on my own. There are 80 million gamblers in the United States and less than 2% know what they are doing. People want to learn how to make their money last longer and have more fun."

Sales Patterns

"I thought my first book, *Casino Gambling Made Easier*, would die, but it's been out for more than three years now," Gayle says. "I had a good summer in 1998, but I had a horrible month in October and sales dropped off dramatically. I was busy with the second book, *More Casino Gambling Made Easier*, but then I got the bright idea of selling those two books together as a set, and boom! 70% of my sales became for the set."

Gayle used the set idea to boost sales of her next two books, *Video Poker Made Easier* and *All Slot Made Easier*. "We decided to offer the slots and video poker books with a set of four laminated strategy cards and the casino gambling tips booklets. To distinguish this set of books from the first set, we called it our Premium Offer. Now the Premium Offer is our biggest seller."

Although direct sales to consumers for the first two books have dropped off, they now sell better than ever through the three largest Internet bookstores, Amazon.com, BarnesandNoble.com, and Borders.com. "Plus Baker & Taylor buys our books now, on our terms, because the original books have a market with libraries."

Gayle is still concerned about having sales dry up and being stuck with unsold books. Printing thousands of books at one time and then trying to sell them makes this seasoned gambler nervous. "I'm looking at print-on-demand. Even if I have to pay $3.00 per book my margins are good enough that I'll make an acceptable profit."

Trading Articles for Advertising Space

Gayle's second biggest source of sales after radio interviews is writing articles in exchange for advertising. "I've been writing for *Chance* magazine since they came out in 1996. I write an article for each issue and in exchange they give me a half page ad that would normally cost $3,000 or more."

When a magazine is going to run just one article, Gayle only requires them to get her byline right so interested people can order her books or get more information. "I have a whole list of articles so the editor can pick and choose. There are twenty-one articles from my second book and as many as that from my first book including excerpts.

"But if they want two or more articles, then I want advertising space," Gayle says. She always gets a contract that specifies the details of her agreement with the magazine. Currently she is a contributing editor for ten different publications.

Other Marketing Activities

"I budget anywhere from $100-$200 per month to send direct mailings to previous customers to let them know a new book has come out." Gayle has also participated in three co-op mailings sent by PMA to potential reviewers. Each time she's gotten over fifteen requests for more information, including a high of twenty-nine requests.

One of her most successful ideas was to offer one of her tip cards through *Freebies* magazine. "I offered to send a free slot tip card if a reader sent me a SASE. I got 8,000 replies." In addition to stuffing the card in the envelopes, Gayle included a reply envelope and an order form telling the reader about her first book. "I sold close to 400 books."

Next Gayle offered a free video poker tip card through the same magazine. "I got 6,800 responses, and sold a little less than 300 books." Her response rate was approximately the same for both of the mailings, about 4%.

She's also done well working with *Bottom Line PERSONAL* magazine. "Their readership is over 1,000,000. The magazine comes out twice a month. They offer my tips booklets in their 'Send For' column for $1.00 plus SASE, and the response has been overwhelming. In September 1999 the first offer of the *101 Casino Gambling Tips* booklet brought in over 6,000 replies. In early January 2000 the *101 Slots Tips* booklet did even better."

Gayle is enthusiastic about using booklets to market her books. "I had no idea how much gamblers would love these little booklets. They are pocket sized so they can carry them to casinos. And they sell the books. The *101 Slots Tips* booklet brings in orders for *All Slots Made Easier* and my Premium Offer, while the *101 Casino Gambling Tips* booklet brings in orders for my first two books. I'm about to offer a *101 Video Poker Tips* booklet, and I expect it to sell copies of my book, *Video Poker Made Easier*.

The booklets consist of tips Gayle takes from her books. She found information on putting together booklets by visiting Paulette Ensign's web site for Tips Products International at www.tipsbooklets.com. "I put *101 Casino Gambling Tips* in her e-booklet catalog, and I'm waiting to see how the sales turn out."

Gayle has only done one book signing. She spoke for 1 1/2 hours about casino tips. "It worked out really great. I delivered a dozen copies to the bookstore. They sold them plus another eight copies. About twenty people came, and I sold eight or nine copies at the signing itself."

Putting Up a Web Site

Gayle decided she needed an Internet presence after she had accumulated a reasonable number of products she could sell online. "I had just completed my second book, *More Casino Gambling Made Easier*, plus a single game book of my favorite casino game, *Video Poker Made Easier*. Plus I had a four card set of laminated strategy cards for video poker, slots, and the top Vegas casinos."

With four products to offer, Gayle began to educate herself. "I signed up for as many related e-zines as I could that offered free help. Bookzone hosts our site and provided promotional aids and suggestions to improve it. And I believe that you must offer something free; most surfers expect that on the web. So I put together a free report, *10 Best Casino Gambling Bet/Games*, for surfers to print out plus a page that offers free gaming tips."

Gayle includes testimonials from readers and a company mission statement on her home page. Every page lists complete contact information including mailing address, toll free number and e-mail address. To drive traffic to her site, she writes for numerous online publications.

"You should e-mail the e-zines and tell them about your availability to write articles and ask them to consider a sample of your writing at your web site," Gayle advises. "Once your web presence is established, writing assignments will come your way. Plus I-Syndicate and Talent Direct list authors.

"You should spend at least one hour per day promoting, retooling, or gathering additional marketing tips to build the traffic to your site. Plus remember that your e-mail signature is the best advertising for you and your web site. My e-mail signature not only mentions our URL, mailing address and new product/special pricing announcements, but offers publishers' articles and excerpts."

Gayle believes in plenty of links. "A links page to similar sites will increase traffic to your site. You should provide links to your articles in e-zines and links to free offers or freebie sites. You should also link Amazon.com, bn.com, and Borders.com to your site. Links can bring in more traffic than search engine submissions. I ask radio stations that interview me to add a link from their sites to mine - these can stay up for months."

Looking at her monthly hits report, Gayle says that most visits to her site come from the reciprocal links she has set up. "Sales average about $700 a month, so my web site is paying off. Bundling products together for a total reduced price increases sales. Our most popular product is our premium offer for the slots and video poker books with the strategy cards and tips booklet for $25.00. Our average web sale is higher than sales on the toll free number. I think it's because people can see pictures of our products and get a better description of them, plus we entice them with special bonus offers."

Gayle offers the best prices online for her products. "You should make sure that the prices at your web site are lower than anywhere else on the web so browsers who comparison shop will order through you."

Increasing orders through her web site is a key part of Gayle's future promotional plans. "Expanding our web site is a marketing avenue we plan to explore. We have ten items in our product line now, and plan to offer all five of the tips booklets in downloadable e-format. The idea of doing a discussion group or an e-zine is on the drawing board."

Producing Her Book

"My editor does the typesetting as well as the editing. I found her when I was reading some publication. Her name is Sharon Saunders, and I really enjoy working with her."

The first book initially had a bad cover. "It was really ugly. Red and black. Then for the second printing I went to the large graphic school here in Phoenix and set up a contest for my second cover with a $250 prize. I got twelve entries for my cover from the senior students. One or two entries were throwaways, but it was hard to pick among the rest."

Gayle worked with the young man who won the contest and had him make some changes. She wanted a Canadian $2.00 bill on the cover to pull in her Canadian heritage, and he put the cover on disk for her to send to the printer.

Her first print run was for 1,000 copies. When sales of the books proved to be much easier and faster than for the tapes, she reprinted with a 5,000 print run. Her third printing was for 10,000 copies which included 3,000 books pre-sold to a Canadian catalog company. "Regal Greetings & Gifts is the largest catalog mailing house in Canada. I paid $.70 per copy for that print run, and I sold them to Regal for $4.00. I think that was cheap, but the exchange rate was bad at the time.

"I'm going to try putting out smaller books on just one game and see how they sell. I ran 100 copies of *Video Poker Made Easier* as a test, and people bought that sixty page book for $9.95. A lot of people don't want to bother reading about anything except the game they like."

Before she wrote her second book, Gayle sent out 2,000 questionnaires to people who had ordered the first book, and asked them what else they needed to know. Many people responded. In addition to giving her lots of feedback, they provided her with numerous complimentary quotes. "I dedicated my second book to my readers," Gayle says. Besides including the results of her readers' survey, she printed three pages of their praise comments at the front of the book.

Gayle's choice of sales outlets has kept her return rate to a remarkably low level. "Personally I've only had three books come back from consumers. Twice the cover was wrecked. I sent them back and said they were not in resalable condition. This was after selling 15,000 copies of the first book and 2,000 copies of the second one."

Family Support

"I'm an optimist, but I have my down days," Gayle acknowledges. "Fortunately I've had total support from my husband. And my daughter has always encouraged me to go for my dream. My son and daughter-in-law even tried to distribute my books in Canada, but the tax rules are enough to kill you up there so that didn't work."

She works more than the standard forty hours per week. "I spend 2-3 hours on fulfillment per day, lots of time on the Internet, and 1-2 hours reading. I subscribe to a couple of e-zines and a top seven success tips publication which is sent every day. Plus I write gambling articles or work on another book for 1-2 hours."

"I also spend at least two hours per day calling or faxing or e-mailing to promote my books. I get really upset at people who don't call me back. I've had to learn to be patient despite my type A personality."

Words of Advice

"My books sell well because they are a really easy read. I stayed away from the charts and the percentages. My first book was geared toward women, but I've been pleasantly surprised that sales of my book are 60% to women and 40% to men. Senior men are the hardest to sell." Gayle feels she fills a niche. "I'm the only recognized female casino expert who is credible."

Gayle believes that would-be publishers should do their research first. "Definitely read the books out there on self-publishing. Don't think about doing anything until you have. You should have six months income as back-up, and try a small print run first. I particularly liked John Kremer's book, *1001 Ways to Market Your Book.*

"If you are going to borrow money, second mortgages on your house are cheaper than credit cards," Gayle advises, though she went the credit card route herself. "I got really scared reading that it would cost $12,000 to produce my book, but I did it with about $5,000. I financed it using my credit cards because they wouldn't talk to me at the bank. Plus I thought I could pay this money back real fast. I took a gamble - that's what my life is about."

Her worst financial decision was getting involved with a public relations company who wanted $5,000 to market her book. "I paid about $1,000 out front, and they kept telling me to be patient because we weren't getting results."

Gayle decided to cancel her contract. "I'd put it on my credit card so I got some of that up front money back. I thought I could do a lot more with that $5,000 myself than they were doing, and I did."

In addition to publishing her own books, Gayle is willing to look at other authors' manuscripts, but only if they deal with the two topics she cares to publish. "They would have to be about gambling, or possibly travel. Otherwise I'm not interested."

Chapter Twelve

Selling to New York for Six Figures

Gordon Miller approached the self-publication of his book *Quit Your Job Often and Get Big Raises* the same way as someone would take up snowboarding or planting a garden. "It was fun. I saw this project as kind of a hobby." Unbeknown to Gordon, he was setting into motion a series of events that would lead not to just a different job, but to a complete switch in his career path.

The idea to write a book came to Gordon when he called a buddy to let him know that he had changed jobs. It was the fourth change in less than six years. "I wanted to give him my new phone number, and he told me I was nuts to change jobs so often. I agreed he might be right, but these people kept giving me raises, stock options, and signing bonuses. I got a huge raise each time I changed jobs. I mean, I was shocked at how big the raises were. My buddy told me I ought to write a book about what I was doing.

"I sat down at the computer and started to bang it out. It doesn't take much to do 100 pages, especially when you're telling your own story. It's not like I was writing fiction and had to dream something up."

Gordon sent out about 25 query letters to agents and publishers, and quickly learned how difficult it is to break into print.

"It became apparent that there was very little chance I was going to get my manuscript bought by a publishing company. Unless you are a known personality like an actor or politician or rock star, the chances of getting a first book picked up by a publisher are almost non-existent.

"So I went to a Barnes & Noble store and to the Tattered Cover, and read books about self-publishing. I was kind of soaking up the information and having fun doing it, and that's when I made the decision to go ahead and self-publish."

His corporate experience shaped the way Gordon approached publishing his book. "When you are in a corporation and you are thinking about a major project or a new product offering, whatever, then due diligence and research are key components. I applied those same principles to self-publishing. I had to know a lot more than what I did if I was going to have a chance of being successful. Like with anything else, there are a thousand opinions as to what is the right way to do it. I had to take all the information I was able to learn and decide what I was going to do with it.

"I talked to anybody who knew anything about the book business and I went to seminars. I also talked with the business book buyer at the Tattered Cover. I'd buy him a cup of coffee or just stand there and chat with him for five to ten minutes. I'd never take too much of his time, and he gave me great little morsels of information."

Gordon considered the money he spent educating himself the same as the cost involved in taking up any new hobby. "You know how when you start a hobby, you invest money in equipment. That's what I was doing, investing money to publish this book. I bought about half a dozen books and attended some seminars. I spent a few hundred dollars at the most."

To actually produce the book required an additional investment. "My vision for the book was a cross between the *One Minute Manager* and *Dilbert*. I wanted it to be easy to read and have a cartoon character." Gordon hired a Denver company, Scharf Services, to do the cover and draw the cartoons for his book. He modeled his interior design on the *One Minute Manager.*

"I went to the printer and said I wanted my print to be the same as their print, same size, same number of words per line, and then I priced it for the same price, $9.95, because I didn't think I could get any more than $9.95 for such a small book." The costs for the cover, cartoons, and printing combined came close to $2,000.

Gordon approached his first print run cautiously. "I made the decision to print only 250 copies. I had this fear that if I went out and published 3,000 or 5,000 copies that the book would never sell, and then they would be sitting in my garage. I knew it cost a lot more to print each copy when printing small quantities, but it didn't matter that it was two to three times the cost per book because I was concerned about the total. I thought of those first 250 books not as inventory to sell, but in essence as my advertising budget instead."

Alhough Gordon started off small, he had a hazy plan for a bigger future. "As a result of my research I made the decision to focus on the Denver market. I liked the idea of doing something in small controllable steps where I could really keep my arms around the whole process. That had been my experience in corporate America.

"I knew in the beginning I would be a nobody nationally, but I felt if I could get the book to be successful in Denver, get it selling well, get some publicity and maybe even make a best seller list, I could go regional or even national at some point. My local success would be my springboard to bigger markets."

Saturation Marketing

Based on his business experience, it seemed natural to Gordon to begin promoting his book before he even had copies to sell. "I started the marketing about 45 days before the book was

184 Make Money Self-Publishing

actually printed. I had been in the computer business the last few years before writing this book, and the reps would visit 90 days before a product was coming out to start pitching it, getting people excited, so that's what I did. I went into the bookstores, and I sent letters to the radio stations and TV stations and the newspapers that this book was coming and told them the subject matter."

That fact that most people weren't interested in Gordon or his book didn't discourage him. "Percentage wise maybe 10% of the people got back to me, but that was enough. I figured I needed just two to three successes. If I got a radio station, a TV station, or a newspaper to publish something, I could use that to get the next bit of publicity.

"I did a combination of voice mail messages, letters, and actual visits where I would just stop at places, mainly bookstores, but I also went to a couple of TV and radio stations. I would talk to the person at the front desk and say, 'I don't know how to do this. Who would I talk to and what is the right approach to take with them? Do they like to get letters, voice mail?' Most people were really great.

"When I got my 250 copies it was the classic story. I threw them in the truck and just went from place to place for a week or two during my lunch breaks or in the evenings. I'd say, 'Here is your complimentary copy of the book I was talking about. Tell me what you think about it, tell me if you like it, if it's something your readers would be interested in. Do you think we could do a seminar, a book signing?'

"This approach was effective because I had a contact in each of these bookstores who knew me, had decided I was okay, and liked it that I had asked them for their feedback. I visited somewhere between 30 and 40 stores."

Though Gordon had never listened much to talk radio before, he started to turn it on every time he was in the car so he could decide if they would be interested in interviewing him. "KTLK seemed like a logical choice because it was a business only talk show. They were always talking about the tight labor market and how that was impacting companies. I had sent them a letter, and when the book came out I dropped them a copy. They called me about a week later and scheduled me to be interviewed on the show.

"The good news that came out of that, and this is just a stroke of luck, was they loved the interview so much that they asked me to come back each week as a guest on their show. It was totally lucky, but if you go out and do something, you'd be surprised at what will happen to you."

In addition to gaining a regular radio spot that allowed him to promote his book, Gordon got his first television exposure. "The guy who was the personality on KTLK was also the business reporter on Channel Four TV. After about the second or third time on the radio he asked me to be on Channel Four."

Crowded Booksignings

In the meantime Gordon was doing book signings. "Everybody said that they are a total waste of time, but my book is about telling people how they can make a lot more money at work if they change jobs often, so people came. They wanted to know, is this guy for real or is he a kook?

"My initial book signing was at a Barnes & Noble. The community relations manager, Carol Flagstaff, was one of the first ones to call me back and say she wanted me to do a seminar. She promoted the heck out of it. She put signs in the window and placards in the store, she had it in her newsletter, and we had about fifty people and sold 38 books. It got me really excited about doing a lot more book signings."

Gordon did book signings up and down the Colorado Front Range at most of the major bookstores. No one worried about the fact that he was doing signings at competitors' stores. "They were so jazzed that they didn't care. By that time I was on the Tattered Cover best seller list.

"That turned out to be a huge thing. I had always thought it would be, that it would help me get publicity, other press, help me get into other bookstores or even go regional or national. It was great to go to these bookstores and say, 'I am on every Thursday on KTLK, I have been on Channel Four three times already and am scheduled for several more appearances, and I have been written up in *The Denver Post* and *The Rocky Mountain News*."

Coverage by the Press

Gordon managed to get coverage in the written press by carefully examining the two major Denver metro newspapers for a space that would work for him and his message. "I was doing my due diligence and seeing where I might fit in. When I looked at the Sunday Books & Author section, I thought no way am I going to get in there. They put in real literary books, and my book is a quirky little career book. So I looked at the business section of *The Denver Post*. During the week that section is very hardcore business, but on Sunday they take a more personal approach. I learned this by reading the paper intently.

"They had a column called Vox Pop. It's an opportunity for anybody to submit to *The Post* a previously unpublished, business related item. I wrote a column on strategic job jumping which is the concept in *Quit Your Job Often*. I wrote it in a business-like manner, not as quirky as in my book, and they published it.

"Then I went to *The Rocky Mountain News* and said I have been on KTLK, Channel 4, and published in *The Denver Post*. Would you be interested in doing something with my book? They said okay, send us a copy. About two weeks later the business editor did a column in their Sunday Section talking about new books, and mine was one of three books that he reviewed."

Clearly Gordon's initial print run of 250 books was not enough to meet the demand he was creating. Since he had intentionally printed his books by a technique called Docutec, he was able to reprint another 3,500 copies very quickly, if not economically.

"I was interested in the speed of production, not if I could save $.50 or $1.00 per book. I wasn't seeing this as a main source of income, more as a hobby that was maybe going to become something more. I was starting to think it had the potential to be something larger, and people were telling me that the book could be national. But I wanted to focus on Denver as long as I could and really build a track record there."

Quit Your Job Often first reached bookstores in early May, 1998. Gordon enjoyed all the promotional work he was doing and had achieved impressive results. The combination of the two led to the idea of quitting his full-time corporate job and focusing on his rapidly growing 'hobby'.

"All of my friends and my wife were saying, 'You are really good at this and you ought to go for it.' My kids were out of college, my house was paid for, and I had obviously proven that I didn't have any problem getting a job. My wife and I sat down one night, and she was the one encouraging me to quit.

"And quite frankly, I had been in corporate America for 25 years and I was burnt out. She said quit your job and give it 90 or 120 days and see what happens. If it doesn't work out, you can always get a job again." Open to a new work experience, Gordon gave his notice to his boss in mid June.

Getting the Call

By the first part of July *Quit Your Job Often* had been on the Tattered Cover's business bestseller list for six straight weeks, selling somewhere between forty and fifty copies each week. "Then I got a call from a McGraw Hill senior editor. Their sales rep in the area had been talking to the business book buyer at the Cherry Creek Tattered Cover store. The rep had found out about my book when he asked if the buyer had seen any hot new self-published books."

Getting a call from a New York editor was an incredible experience for Gordon. "I was so ecstatic I could hardly talk to her. It was my big dream that some publisher would come along and buy the book, but I still thought something like that was a pretty remote possibility. The editor said she had heard that my book was doing well and they wanted to see a copy. Could I overnight it to them? They had a space in their catalog and they thought my book might fit in well. They wanted to talk to me about it. Of course I sent them the book.

"They called about two days later to say they had read it, they loved it, and they wanted to negotiate to buy it. I told them I had never done this before and was probably going to find an agent. They said that was a good idea, and we'll get back to you in a couple of days. But I had no idea who my agent was going to be."

Fortunately for Gordon, he didn't have to spend much time looking. "That morning I picked up *The Denver Post* and on the inside front cover I saw a column about a local agent named Jody Rein who had just won an advance in the mid six figures for a Denver author's book.

"I picked up the phone and called her. I left a message that said, 'This is Gordon Miller. I have just written a book called *Quit Your Job Often* and here's what has happened. It's been on the Tattered Cover best seller list, I have been on KTLK, Channel 4, in *The Denver Post* and *The Rocky Mountain News*, and now McGraw Hill is calling me. Would you be interested in talking about this?'

"She called me back that afternoon and told me to overnight her the book. She called again the next morning and said, 'Let's get together and talk.' She was pretty conservative in her approach. She thought it was kind of early in the game to be talking with the New York houses."

Jody believed it might be better to wait a little longer to give the book time to develop a stronger history of increasing sales, but the interest was high. "She told me that if the track record of sales continued another two to three months, then we'd have something to talk about with the editors, but she got on the phone anyway with some other publishers. Twelve of them were interested in the book.

"Over the next two weeks she had conversations with all of them and we decided that the interest level was so high that we set the mark at what it would take to buy the book. We said here is the level that you have to play at if you want to play with us. If you are willing to pay at least $100,000 for the rights to this book, you can play. Four were willing to do that. It was very exciting. We knew we had at least $100,000."

Gordon was thrilled to watch as Jody set up what is called a best and final offer. "The four finalists were to submit their best offer to buy the rights to *Quit Your Job Often* without there being any specifications except for the $100,000. They could be creative and say we'll give him $100,000 and send him on a national tour in our private Lear jet, whatever they wanted to try to win the deal. Doubleday came back with a two book offer with a combined advance of $250,000 for *Quit Your Job Often* and the promise of a second book."

Doubleday kept Gordon's first book basically the same as his self-published version. "They made some enhancements to the internal graphics of the book. I had heard all the horror stories about how publishers ruin books, but they were just the opposite. I worked very closely with them as they had said in their proposal that they would allow me to do. They said they were only making suggestions, and if there was anything I didn't like, they wouldn't do it. And they didn't.

"We edited the whole book and they made positive changes. They standardized bold print, put a page line at the bottom of each page, just small graphical things that made the book look more professional. They wanted to keep the cover intact because obviously it had been successful, and why tinker with success? They were incredibly wonderful."

Though Doubleday bought the rights in the summer of 1998, they intentionally delayed their edition until January, 1999. "They wanted to roll it out at the first of the year because that's the time people think about their careers and about changing jobs. That's when the head of publicity wanted to get me out in front of the press."

Doubleday assigned a company publicist to work with Gordon. "I interviewed live on about sixty radio stations in the first half of 1999, but some of them simulcast to multiple stations so I've been on 351 radio stations. Doubleday has a tracking service that gives them reports so that's how I know the total numbers. I was on CNN in January and on Fox News, and had numerous television appearances in New York City."

The initial Doubleday print run was 25,000 copies, and the second print run was 50,000. Though Gordon continued to promote his first book, his contract with them specified that he deliver a second completed manuscript by June, 1999. He took a brief break from promoting *Quit Your Job Often* while he wrote that book.

Gordon plans to write additional books. " I have something like eight career-oriented books conceptualized already, a series of business books. Maybe my next few books will go through Doubleday, but there will probably be a time when I self-publish again in addition to working with a big publisher, because I loved doing it. I loved doing the cover, going to the printer and checking the press run, putting the books in my car and driving them around. I was like a little kid. I absolutely loved it. I would self-publish again purely for the experience."

Chapter Thirteen

Hiking and Publishing for a Living

No matter how enthusiastic most hikers are about their favorite pastime, they must fit their hiking trips into short weekends or the occasional week or two-week long vacation. Hiking is their hobby; they need real jobs to earn the money for the outdoor gear and all of life's other necessities.

When Rich and Sue Freeman took sabbaticals from their jobs so they could walk the entire length of the Appalachian Trail, they thought they were taking a once-in-a-lifetime special holiday. But during their trip they were forced by circumstances to rethink their work lives.

"We just wanted to take a break from the rat race," Rich explains. "Six months off to hike the Appalachian Trail." He and Sue arranged their sabbaticals and organized everything they needed for their mini-adventure. Then, a month before they were scheduled to leave, Rich's boss called him to say his company had changed its mind.

"He told me that if I took the sabbatical I would be literally walking away from the company. Sue and I talked it over. I was a manager of customer service for the Eastman Kodak company and making a good income, but at that point I had had enough. I was burnt out and tired from all the downsizing. We figured we still had Sue's career going, and we could certainly live on her income. So I left my job – a twenty-three-year career."

During their hike Sue kept in touch with her company, Johnson & Johnson. Soon she began to get inklings that they were going through a downsizing process also. "They laid off my boss, the vice-president of marketing, and all of my peers, so the writing was on the wall that I wouldn't have my job when I came back."

When they arrived home that fall, they were both unemployed. "Because we had lived for six months with everything we really needed on our backs, and had a wonderful time, we knew we owned too many material things," Rich says. "Not having jobs was an opportunity, not a disaster. We had savings."

The Freemans had read the book *Your Money or Your Life* by Joe Dominguez and Vicki Robin, and were inspired at the idea of living in a way that reflected their deepest values and interest. So instead of panicking at the loss of their corporate jobs, they decided to simplify. "Reading that book is what started us on this whole path, " Sue says. "I absolutely recommend it."

When they evaluated their options they realized that what they most liked to do was hike and they wanted to share that joy with others. Since most people couldn't take six months off to go hiking, the Freemans decided to look for short hiking trails around Rochester, New York, that people could enjoy in the span of an evening. They would describe these trails in a book and sell it through local stores.

"We had never published before, but we had learned on the trail that anything you want to do, you can do. Just do it one step at a time," Rich says. Sue checked out numerous books from the library on how to publish including John Kremer's book on marketing and Dan Poynter's manual on the basics of self-publishing.

"We printed 2,000 copies of our first book, *Take a Hike! Family Walks in the Rochester Area*, and it sold out in four months," Sue says. "Our first book has been our best seller by far. We made a profit that first year. Our earnings, sales minus expenses, were about $20,000. We were happy."

The Freemans now realize that most first books don't do as well as their initial book. "We were very lucky," Rich says, "but our sales made us overconfident for our other books. We then learned some lessons about printing too many copies."

Making a Living and Cutting Costs

Their first book came out in June of 1997. "I didn't send out any galleys," Sue says. "Being a regional book we didn't need to get into the big review publications. We sell mostly to locals, families with kids who want to get out hiking, people who are new to the community and even people who have lived here all their lives. These trails have been built within the last eight years so many people didn't know they existed. We've gotten a really good reception."

Rich says, "We thought sales would drop after Christmas, but for some reason they didn't. I still don't understand why not. We're on the fourth printing of our first title and we've sold about 8,000 copies." The book continues to sell 1,000 copies per year. "I expect our sales of this book to drop at some point, but never to stop. New people keep moving to Rochester."

"We are living off what we earn now," Sue says. "But I would like to be able to add a little more into savings for our retirement like we used to do. Plus, periodically, we are going to come up with expenses we need to cover. So we need a little more income, but not much more."

Rich and Sue have eliminated some of their expenses to make it easier for them to live on a reduced income. "We came back from the Appalachian Trail to all of our toys and a custom built home that Sue had designed. We've been trying to get rid of that stuff. We sold the new cars and my ultra light airplane. We sold the house and we rent for now."

"We will probably buy a house again," Sue adds, "but something very inexpensive. We don't want to work to support our house. The more debt you have, the more income you need to support it."

Their frugality extends to their business expenses as well. "The key for anyone who wants to be profitable in this business is to keep costs as low as you can," Sue explains. The Freemans do all of their book production except the copy editing, cover designs, and the binding and printing. They work out of their home and store their inventory there as well.

They paid for the copy editing of their first book via barter, by exchanging home repair for copy editing done by an ex-employee. They hired a friend who is a graphic artist to do their cover. "I went in with an idea of what I wanted for a design and she put it together for me," Rich says. "We paid her a really minimal amount."

Dividing Their Responsibilities

Working closely with a spouse isn't for every couple, but Rich and Sue were confident it would work for them. Hiking the Appalachian Trail had turned out to be a pretest of their ability to spend a lot of time together. "Living with someone else within a six-foot distance, twenty-four hours a day, was one of the things that prepared us," Rich says.

Even so, they make a point to create time apart. "We need to take breaks periodically," Sue says. "I take a water aerobics class, different things like that to get away and meet other people."

"We also divvy up the publishing chores," Rich says. "When it comes to drawing maps, I'm the boss for that. Sue's background is in marketing so when it comes to that, she is the boss." Sue handles getting publicity through press releases and cooperative ads, while Rich is the one who goes out on sales calls to local businesses.

During the summer they spend most of their time hiking. "We go out for two to three days at a time. When we come back we sit down and Sue writes a rough draft and I do the maps. Then we'll exchange everything back and forth to proof it for the first time. When we are all done with hiking in the late fall we begin the process of putting the book together."

Taking notes has actually added to their enjoyment when they go hiking. "It makes us pay more attention to our surroundings," Sue says. "We're more consciously observant. Having to cover the trails for the books becomes an excuse that forces us to get outside and explore without feeling guilty about it. We call it work, but it's 99% fun."

Their work is also their exercise. "Often people find it difficult to set aside time to exercise or to get outdoors for enjoyment. Since we combine it with what is technically 'work', we make sure we get out more. It's playing with a dual purpose."

A Little of This and a Little of That

Selling their books requires the Freemans to constantly look for promotional opportunities. "I send review copies to people at the local magazines and newspapers," Sue says. "We got relatively good coverage the first year in the summer guides that the different magazines and newspapers produce. Rich and I did something unique with our lives, so it was real easy. They liked covering the fact that we left corporate America and hiked the Appalachian Trail."

"Reviews will create sales for the next week, and then they immediately drop off again," Rich explains. "We have to continually be in some article. Sue is always trying to plug the book, and we are on radio quite a bit and on TV every once in a while. But even then, people still haven't heard of us. It's a constant effort. We thought that writing the books, getting them printed, and out to the stores would be the major portion of the publishing business, and it turns out to be 40%. The rest is promotion. You think you have covered the market, but you keep finding other areas that haven't heard of you."

Sue is always thinking of different angles to get into the newspapers again. "Winter will come and I'll write about cross country skiing. Or I'll write about using the trails for dog walking or learning the history of the railroad beds.

"I've done a lot of cooperative advertising with the local hiking clubs and humane society. I don't pay them anything to run my ad in their newsletter, but I give them $5.00 for every book that is sold. It's worked especially well."

In 1999 Sue scored a marketing hit with a health maintenance organization. "I was able to get our local HMO to run a coupon for 10% discount and free shipping in their newsletter. The coupon ran just before Christmas and orders began to come in quickly."

To make it easy for local merchants to decide to try their books, Rich buys plastic and makes it into display stands for their books. "It costs me $1.25 to make the stands. If I bought them instead it would be $6.00 apiece. A counter display stand holds six books and tilts them at an angle. When I go into a store I give them the stand so they can display the books prominently and encourage impulse purchases. Many stores have displayed them right on the checkout counter." The books are placed in new stores on a returnable basis. "They have nothing to lose," says Rich. "If the books don't sell, we take them back, no hassle."

Though he doesn't like being a salesperson, Rich believes in his product. "I know the retailers are going to make money on the books because they are a quality product. And though doing sales isn't what I would choose to do in life, I think, 'Gee, do I want to eat next week?' Nobody is going to come knock on my door, so I knock on their doors."

"Not everyone says yes," Sue cautions. "People don't say no, either. They say, 'Let me think about it,' like the museum gift shops who make excuses and give you the run around. Sometimes we have to find somebody with an in with a museum. They tell us, 'Let me talk to that person,' and then we have success. It's who you know."

"What's exasperating is going to a national company," Rich says. "Their buyer is national, and they aren't going to deal with someone who can sell to only three of their stores, even if the product would fit really well." He has had his best luck placing books with the strictly local stores including gas stations, gift shops, hiking and biking stores, and bird shops. These type of stores have consistently accounted for 31-35% of their total sales during their first three years as publishers.

One aspect of marketing that drives Sue crazy is her inability to track which marketing activity produces the best results. "I will run an article in a local magazine, and some people will call us and say, 'I heard about you in the *Lake Affect* magazine.' That makes me feel good because I actually produced some results, but so often they read about our books and I don't know the direct correlation with them coming into a bookstore and buying a book."

Rich submitted their web site to a local TV station's web site that highlights other web sites. "It's a local news station and they have the weather, the local news, and movie theaters. We are up to thirty people a day visiting our site. I am certain this promotes book sales, but how many? We don't know. Nobody has called us to buy a book and said they saw us on the WOKR web site."

Sue has also gone to trailheads to put flyers under the windshield wipers of the cars parked there. "The flyer gives people the option of going into our web site and ordering via credit card or mailing a check to us. But they can also go into Barnes & Noble. I never know if they did that instead of ordering directly from us."

Rich fully appreciates the direct sales. Though they are only 5% of their business, they are the most profitable sales because they circumvent the middlemen. One of Sue's most successful press releases was to an automobile club detailing ten different sights around the Rochester area that people could see if they hiked the trails mentioned in their books. "The club ran the release for free. It had our web site address and phone number, and the phone rang off the hook with sales."

Sue isn't keen on library conventions as a way to sell to libraries. "There was one in Rochester and I went just to observe, and my impression was that the people weren't looking to see what books were available. I don't think that's how librarians do their shopping. But I am in a cooperative program with other local authors to do a mailing to all the libraries in our region."

The Rochester library is their biggest library customer. "The main library orders for all the other library branches, and there are 30 to 40 branches," Rich says. "They can track how often a book is checked out, and if there is the demand for them, they will have four to five copies in each branch." With five books published, the Freemans have sold 290 copies to the libraries located in the central and western part of the state of New York.

Including an order form in the back of their books has resulted in sales for the Freemans. "I have gotten a fair share of orders that way," Sue says. "Out of 10,000 books sold I have probably gotten 30 orders that way. It doesn't sound like much, but it's 30 more direct orders than I would have gotten otherwise. A little bit here, a little bit there, and it all adds up."

The Freemans are also trying to encourage sales for multiple copies of their titles. "One insurance agent buys books in quantity and gives them as gifts to his customers," Sue says. "We have a program ready to roll out this spring which is a mailing to real estate agents suggesting our books as a gift for their clients when they close on a house."

Book Signings

The Freemans have arranged numerous book signings. "They don't move a lot of copies," Sue says, "but the bookstore usually puts the book on a table with a sign about the upcoming book signing. It's more exposure than anything else, getting the name of the book in the store's newsletter for a month."

"It's one of the most boring things you could ever do," Rich admits, "but at the same time we are talking with the managers of the stores. They see that you are trying to help make money for them, too, and now we notice that bookstores display our books face out."

"We try to do some kind of slide show and presentation," Sue says. "Or around Christmas time we talk the mall bookstores into putting a table in front of the store entrance. We talk to people as they go by and encourage them to make impulse purchases. That's been pretty successful. If the mall is in the more affluent areas we can sell 20 books in an hour or two.

"For regular book signings we've found that some stores don't do a lot of promotion. Once we traveled down to the southern tier of the state to do a slide show on our book, and the store had done absolutely nothing. They had some employee turnover and the signing fell through the cracks. No one was there; it was a disaster.

"Then there are stores like Borders Books & Music. They asked us for a mailing list. I gave them names and addresses of people that bought our first book, *Take a Hike!*, and they sent postcards to all of these people. It was wonderful free promotion for us." Sue now sends out her own press releases instead of assuming the stores will do it.

Sometimes one of their customers will surprise them at a book signing. "After a slide show on area hiking trails that we presented at a Borders store, a lady came up to us with a three ring binder and asked for our signatures," Sue says. "The binder was full of clippings and pictures from her self-organized hiking club. She and her friends use our books as their exercise guide. Each week they explore a new trail and document their adventures in the binder. I've signed many books, but this was the first hiking club binder I've ever signed."

In order to learn more about the book selling business, Sue and Rich took part-time jobs with a Barnes & Noble store during the first two Christmas seasons they were publishers. "It worked well for us," Rich says. "We got to know everyone in the store, and we learned how bookstores operate."

"We worked in the biggest Barnes & Noble in the city," Sue says, "and they let us put up two huge dumps full of our books in very visible areas." Overall the bookstores have been an important avenue of sales for Footprint Press, accounting for 51%-63% of their sales, depending on the year.

Discovering the Value of the Regional Niche

The Freemans came out with two new titles in the spring of 1998, *Take Your Bike! Family Rides in the Rochester Area* and *Bruce Trail: An Adventure Along the Niagra Escarpment*. They discovered that going biking wasn't as popular as hiking, at least not with book buyers, and they also learned that marketing a national/international book was much more involved than promoting a regional book.

"*Bruce Trail* is very slow selling. We tried to go international with Canada and that has made it difficult to get the right distributor," Rich says. It took them six months before they were picked up by Mother Pickle Distributing in Toronto, and sales significantly improved in the early months of 1999.

Because they believed that the Bruce Trail book would have a broader market than their Rochester guide, they decided to print 4,000 copies instead of their typical 2,000 print run. They thought that if the stores in the area along the Bruce Trail each took one to two books they wouldn't have enough books unless they doubled their print run. Instead they found it a slow slog to get their new title into the stores.

"The difference in turn around time for one of our regional books versus *Bruce Trail* is a year," Rich explains. "For a regional book I could literally drive down to the bookstores and talk to the book buyers, and they would take copies. We would be on TV, Sue would be marketing and promoting the book, and we could do all that within weeks."

"Everything just took longer nationally," Sue says. "We had to give away lots of books because we were trying to reach a larger audience." Instead of giving away a dozen or so review copies as they did for their two regional titles, they sent out over 150 review copies for the *Bruce Trail*, or one review copy for every copy of that title that sold in 1998. In contrast, they sold forty-nine books for each review copy they sent out for *Take Your Bike*.

Trying to ship across the border to Canada was also complicated. "We had lots of problems and costs associated with that, " Rich says, "and then we had the Canadian dollar issue. What happened if they paid us in Canadian dollars? From this book we learned to stay with our genre and our area. We can't compete with the large publishing companies so we need to stick to something that won't interest them, and that's regional books."

Expanding Their List of Titles

Each year they've been in business, the Freemans have netted a larger income. They went from earning a net profit before taxes of just over $20,000 their first year to almost $50,000 their third year. This happened at the same time that their sales figures for each book decreased. For example, *Take a Hike! Rochester* sold 3,900 copies during its first year, 2,700 copies its second year, and 1,300 its third year. In order to increase their income, the Freemans had to expand their list each year, growing from one title to three and then to five. Their new titles for 1999 were *Take a Hike! Family Walks in the Finger Lakes and Genesee Valley Region* and *Take Your Bike! Family Rides In the Finger Lakes and Genessee Valley Region.*

For the year 2000 they scheduled the release of three additional books for their press written by two outside authors. One of the books is very regional while the other two books will cover the entire state of New York. Both writers were given no advance with a promise of 10% royalty on net sales.

"We approached these authors to write these books," Sue explains. "If we're going to live off this business long term, we need to get the revenue up higher than it is right now. One author is the outdoor writer for the local newspaper. We liked his writing style and we had some ideas for books he could write that would be appropriate for us.

"The other author was referred to us. We teach a class on hiking and biking for a company in Rochester that offers programs for people on all kinds of diverse subjects. The company owner referred us to this guy who is an avid birder, and he's working on a book for us on where to go birding around central and western New York state."

Their contracts with these authors specify that they will participate in marketing activities. "They need to be willing to do radio and TV interviews, book signings, and give seminars and talks," Sue says. "A book won't go very far if the author won't promote it."

Working with other authors is more difficult in some ways than writing and publishing their own books. "It complicates the whole process," Sue says. "You have to be careful to communicate at every stage. But our time is limited. We can't be researching, writing new books, plus keep up with the marketing and promotions. Working with other authors is a necessity."

Despite being a new and very small publisher without a listing in the phone book, Footprint Press receives one or two unsolicited manuscript submissions each month. "Most people have no clue whatsoever about what's appropriate to send us," Sue says. Even though their web site, www.footprintpress.com, spells out exactly what types of books they publish, they usually receive anything but what they want. "What most people don't understand, and what we didn't understand ourselves when we first started, is that publishers specialize in different areas."

Resisting Temptation

Sometimes it's been hard for the Freemans to stick to their resolve to limit their company to a manageable size. "We were recently approached by another publisher who was trying to focus his direction and get rid of some outdoor recreation books," Rich recalls. "He had some great color hard copy ready to go to print, and he asked if we wanted to take over the process. They were gorgeous books. I knew the writer and the photographer, and they were absolutely top quality."

The opportunity was tempting, but it presented a dilemma as well. "We had to do some soul searching and say, 'Do we want to continue with our life style? Or are we willing to be office-bound publishers?' Plus we would have had to get into an area that we know nothing about which is color printing, and it would have been a large outlay of money in the beginning."

"We got into this business because we wanted to be able to make a living and enjoy hiking and biking, not because we had a burning desire to be publishers," Sue states firmly. "At that time we were about to take off to hike the Florida Trail, and then half a year later we planned to hike a portion of the Pacific Crest Trail. If we had taken on these other books we would have been tied down to Rochester."

"It started to sound like we were going to be exactly where we were before, working twelve to fourteen hour days trying to keep up with stuff and not being able to take any breaks, " Rich says. "It's hard in this society to not get into being better, bigger, more." But the Freemans had been there, done that. They told the other publisher thank you, but they weren't interested.

Currently, the Freemans work about eight hours per day. "But our work hours are very sporadic," Sue explains. "On average we work from 10:00 a.m. until 6:00 p.m., but we may take off several hours during the day to do a home project or go visit someone. Then we'll work some extra hours in the evening. We aren't tied to any definitive schedule."

They also reserve blocks of time for vacation hikes. "In 1997 we spent five weeks on a long hike plus a month on another vacation. In 1998 we spent two weeks on a long bike trip, plus another month on vacation. In 1999 we planned a five-week hike, but it fell through. We did spend two weeks hiking, though, plus a month in Florida."

Printing Books, Taking Credit Cards & Fulfillment

The Freemans have changed printers each year they've been in business. "Each time we print, I send out fifteen to twenty requests for bids," Sue says. "Our first book was printed by McNaughton and Gunn. The second time we went with Data Reproductions. They had been highly recommended through PMA, and we had really good luck with them. Then this year Bang outbid them. We had heard good things about them, so I had no qualms about switching."

"It just depends on the time of the year and how busy the printers are," Rich explains. "Obviously Bang wasn't busy because they worked on our books right away. We could go back to them in six months with the exact same book and get an entirely different bid."

The Freemans don't have a merchant account for taking credit cards. "We haven't had enough business yet to justify it,"

Sue says. "We use Book Clearing House instead. They charge us 20% of the book price. They take the orders via a 1-800 number, process the credit cards, and then fax the information for us to do the fulfillment. I also call them if somebody wants to order from us, but wants to use a credit card." Credit card orders that come through their web site are processed by CCNow for a fee of 8%.

A number of wholesalers handle orders from the bookstores. "I recommend that people work with as many reputable wholesalers as they can," Sue says. "Most bookstores deal with Ingram, so initially we approached them through their Express program for small publishers. That program was the only one that was financially viable for us.

"We had to send them three or four free copies of our first book and wait a few months before they let us know they would take it. Then they started to fill orders. When I notified them about our new books they actually sent me an order. I don't have to send them the free copies any more."

The Freemans have acquired many of their wholesalers without soliciting them. "We're at the point that we get orders from companies we have never heard of. We look them up on the Internet and verify that they are wholesalers. Then I send them a pro forma that they pay in advance. People on the publishers' list serv say they have successfully asked for prepayment, so we've been asking for that, too."

When the Freemans go on long hikes and are gone for weeks at a time, a family member usually helps out. "When we were in Florida, my brother came over and filled orders," Sue says. "Other times my parents have come up from Florida to do that. We don't have them do any other part of the business except keep the orders flowing."

If the business goes without help for a week or so, Rich remains relaxed about the situation. "These are only hiking books so it's no big deal if things are a little slow and we don't get them out as fast as possible. I hate to lose sales because you know it's money out of your pocket, but at the same time you do what you can."

Advice for New Presses

"Don't pay for advertising," Sue says. "I would have if I weren't on a publishers list serv." She thinks that joining a list serv is valuable both for the advice and the companionship. "I miss the aspect of interacting with other people at work. The list serv helps."

"You have to be good at handling a lot of little details," Rich says. "Publishing is basically project management. You also need to have a good lump sum of cash to start with so you have something to live off. Some lady e-mailed me the other day saying she was starting a small publishing company. She had no money and was looking for funds to start her business. I really discouraged her. She hadn't done the basic research."

Besides learning how the publishing business works, Rich emphasizes the necessity to confirm the market's need for a particular book. "The book has to be about a specific topic. We go to the library and explore the Internet, do a lot of research to find out if there is any other information available on the topic already. We knew there was nothing else out there like our books."

Out of the Rat Race and Loving It

Sue and Rich lead completely different lives now that they've become hiking publishers instead of corporate soldiers. "Our friends and family comment all the time that we look relaxed and happy," Sue says. "We don't set an alarm clock; we simply sleep until we wake up. Then we lie in bed for an hour sipping coffee and reading the newspaper."

Even the daily chores of everyday life are less stressful. "Things like scheduling a doctor's appointment are so much easier," Sue explains. "I used to have to plan well in advance to set time aside on my calendar, then pray that the doctor didn't run late. Now I can go whenever the doctor has a cancellation."

No longer slaves to a day timer, the Freemans follow a more natural rhythm. "We can take off and do something else regardless of the day of the week or the hour," Sue says. "Now we have to look at our watches to tell what day it is."

Chapter Fourteen

Part-Time Publisher, Full-Time Income

An experienced businessman, Kenn Amdahl has owned nightclubs and worked as a commercial real estate broker. "I've owned several businesses, and publishing is by far the easiest one I've tried. Not counting the time spent writing, I work five to ten hours a week. I check my e-mail, pick up orders from the fax, and stick address labels on boxes of books.

"Every three to four months, I head to the Denver Public Library and track down magazines I've never heard of that might review my books. I send out twenty to thirty review copies, and then I don't do anything special again for awhile."

Kenn's low maintenance, part-time approach to his publishing company has resulted in sales of over 40,000 copies of his first book, *There Are No Electrons*, and over 8,000 copies of his second book, *Algebra Unplugged*. Although first year sales for both books were modest, sale numbers per year have increased over time. The growth in sales for his first book was a complete surprise to Kenn.

"I thought *There Are No Electrons* would stop selling. I assumed sales would taper off into nothing within a year. That's what I had been told book sales do. Then I planned to take Clearwater Publishing and drive a stake through its heart. But the orders kept coming."

Kenn originally decided to create his first book as an experiment. He wanted to write something entertaining about a dull subject, and electricity was as dull a subject as he could find. He liked the resulting manuscript, and so did a lot of publishers when he submitted it. "Everyone was nice. I got just dozens of rejection letters from editors saying they loved the book, but they didn't think there was a market for it."

After receiving the eighty-ninth rejection sweetly laced with positive comments, Kenn decided to print a modest 500 copy first print run. He spent about $2,300 for the book production costs plus $300 postage to mail out review copies.

"I sent out 100 copies with no response. I sent out another 100 copies and got two reviews. One was in Southern California, but it didn't do me any good because none of the bookstores there carried the book."

The second review appeared in *Radio Electronics Magazine*, a publication with a national circulation of 250,000. "It was a one column review on a three column page, and it sold out the rest of my first print run. If I had not gotten that one review, *There Are No Electrons* would have died, and that would have been it for me as a publisher."

Modifying the Cover

Even with his initial print run sold out, Kenn hesitated about going back to press. He had almost broken even with expenses and income the first time around. Perhaps he should get out while his losses were small. He did decide to do a second print run, but first he made a change to *There Are No Electrons*.

"People chose not to buy the first printing because of the cover. It was two color and looked a little cartoonish. It didn't stand out from any distance in a bookstore. I decided that if I were going to reprint, I wanted the cover to be startling so it would get people's attention. I thought my market was eighteen to twenty-year-old men, so I wanted a picture of a pretty woman on the cover."

Kenn hired two models, a man to be a wizard at work and a woman to stand by watching him. The female model had a generous bosom, and she selected a dress that was quite revealing. Kenn was concerned that people would think her picture on the cover was exploitative.

"I took it around to different bookstores to get people's reactions. I showed it to a lady bookseller and asked her if she would buy a book with this cover. She said no. But then I asked her if she would carry it in her store. She said, 'Oh, yes,' because she thought it would sell, even though she personally wouldn't buy it."

Her reaction clinched the new cover's fate. "That's when I decided to go with the cleavage. This new cover has sold copies of the book, though it's turned out that my market is actually much broader than I suspected."

Kenn has a unique theory about effective cover design. "I think the cover needs to make people curious to the point where they will hold the book for at least ten seconds. Then it starts to feel like their book, not the bookstore's book. That book then goes home with them." To achieve his ten-second goal he relies on the usual blurbs on the back, but also photographs on the front cover showing people engaged in some activity, whether a wizard experimenting with electricity or teenagers making music.

It's important to Kenn that his covers accurately reflect the contents of his books. He knows that a wizard on the cover of a book about electricity is unusual, "but this is a very quirky book, and it needs a weird cover." The tone of the algebra book is casual rather than academic, and its cover reflects that as well, showing a teen band grouped in front of a graffiti covered wall.

Kenn's books are used as textbooks by companies such as Dow Chemical and by schools, including the American University in Lima, Peru. A lot of home schoolers use his books, and he also sells quite a few through bookstores to adults who want to fill in the gaps in their educations.

Reviews and Other Marketing Activities

The main promotional activity for Clearwater's titles is sending review copies to magazines and newsletters that have tightly targeted audiences. "My most effective review ever appeared in *Monitoring Times*. This is a magazine for people who have scanners so they can listen to the police. The magazine's circulation is only 30,000, but the review sold over 1,000 copies. Its readers wanted to know how electricity works."

Though it's impossible to track the exact number of sales resulting from any particular review, Kenn thinks he has a good idea. "A lot of magazines have a bounce back card. Readers can circle a number if they want more information, and the magazines will send me that card. And readers who send in individual orders will say where they read about my book." He says sales through bookstores are harder to pin down, "but if last month Barnes & Noble bought six copies and this month they buy 150, you can see the correlation with the review that just came out."

While Kenn was writing his math book he slacked off on soliciting reviews for his first title. "Sales of *There Are No Electrons* dropped noticeably." But as Kenn renewed his review copy mailings, sales bounced up again. Despite occasional dips, overall sales of his titles have continued to increase each year.

Another successful promotion involved getting his titles into catalogs. *Algebra Unplugged* has been included in catalogs targeted to math teachers, and *There Are No Electrons* was offered in *The Common Reader*, a small catalog of strange books that is sent to 100,000 people. "They sold 400 copies per year for five years before they dropped the book."

Kenn has also tried direct mail. "I sent out brochures the first year to bookstores and libraries for *There Are No Electrons*, and it resulted in sales. I considered it successful. I'm a bread-on-the-water kind of guy. Making enough sales immediately to pay for the mailings wasn't important to me. I wanted these books out there as my sales force."

Four Keys to Sell Books

"I think four things sell books: the cover, the blurbs on the back, word of month, and reviews. Reviews are the most important in the beginning. Ultimately word of month sells the most books, but you have to sell a certain quantity of books before this kicks in. Now that I've sold over 40,000 copies of *There Are No Electrons*, I don't have to do anything to sell a base number of books every month."

Though Kenn considers blurbs to be the smallest factor in selling a book, he's made a point of acquiring some fantastic quotes. "I got quotes from three or four people for *There Are No Electrons* by sending books to 30 or 40 people. I didn't have any personal connection with them beforehand, but I did write personalized letters to each of them. I tried to make the letter itself entertaining, honest and appropriate."

The angle Kenn used to approach Dave Barry was inspired by a direct mail piece Kenn had received from Dan Quayle. "It said I could join an 'insiders' club with benefits including a Dan Quayle breakfast. Cost of membership? One grand. Dave Barry apparently got the same invitation because he wrote a column about it.

"I wrote him a letter indicating that we 'insiders' should stick together. Therefore if he ever wanted me to write a blurb for him, I'd be happy to do so. And, of course, I hoped he felt the same way."

He did, at least to the extent that he gave Kenn a blurb. "*There Are No Electrons* changed my life," announces Dave Barry on the back of that book. "I lost 17 pounds in five minutes without

214 Make Money Self-Publishing

dieting, and I feel great!" Quotes from people such as Ray Bradbury, Clive Cussler, and George Garrett also appear on the back cover. Another five pages of quotes from favorable reviews are inside the back cover.

The blurbs on the back of *Algebra Unplugged* aren't from famous people, but they do have the weight of authority. For example, "*Algebra Unplugged* is unlike any other mathematics text about algebra. Through the use of creative analogies, the authors explain the areas that are often stumbling blocks for students," states *Mathematics Teaching in the Middle School*.

Kenn plans the size of his print runs so he can take maximum advantage of early, favorable reviews. "The first print run should be small, no more than 3,000 copies, so you can add review quotes to the back cover when you order more books." Sales of the second printing of *Algebra Unplugged* accelerated dramatically, and he believes the addition of the blurbs made the difference.

Foreign and Domestic Rights

Kenn sold the German rights to *There Are No Electrons* to a company called Rohart. "It sold because I had a fan in Germany who is well respected in the industry. He pushed it, but the details were handled by a US agent and German subagent." The sale took about six months to become final.

"I'm happy to sell foreign rights because it doesn't cut into my own income, and it's easy. There really is no downside. Any money I get is extra."

Kenn is not so eager to sell domestic rights. "My agent thinks I could sell the rights to *There Are No Electrons* to a U.S. publisher for a $250,000 advance. Even if she's right, I'm not interested. After paying her fee and maybe a third in taxes, I might end up with $150,000. If I managed to invest that for a 10% return, and that's doubtful, then I'd only get $15,000 per year. I'd rather keep my book."

Other Authors

Kenn wrote *There Are No Electrons* by himself, but he co-wrote *Algebra Unplugged* with a professor of mathematics, Jim Loats, from the Metropolitan State College of Denver. "Co-writing with Jim involved meeting with him every couple of weeks for breakfast so he could explain things I was having trouble with. He wrote some chapters, and I wrote the same chapters in a different way. We wanted each concept explained at least two ways, though I revised his chapters to match the overall tone of the book."

Kenn would like to publish other authors, especially if they have written books that match up well with his current non-fiction titles. "Even though I want books on subjects taught in high school, I get almost exclusively inappropriate submissions instead."

Authors contact Clearwater Publishing about twice a week looking for a publisher. Their approaches range from query letters to phone calls or unsolicited manuscripts in the mail. Ninety percent of the proposed manuscripts are fiction. Kenn's own novel, *The Land of Debris and the Home of Alfredo*, has sold poorly.

"If I were willing to promote myself, I think I could market my fiction," he says, "but I would rather sell my words than my sparkling personality. Non-fiction can be sold through reviews."

Despite his focus on non-fiction, Kenn did try to acquire the rights to an existing story. "I tried to publish a fiction title that had been out of print for twenty years. It was a children's book I loved as a kid. I tracked down the author in New York, but I got beat out by a week. He had just sold the reprint rights to someone else."

Kenn's first release by another author occurred in 2000. *The Barefoot Fisherman* was written by his son, Paul Amdahl. "It's a how-to-fish book written for children," Kenn says. "Jim Fay, the author of *Parenting with Love and Logic*, wrote a fabulous, glowing introduction for it."

Another year 2000 release was *Economics for the Impatient* by Carol Turner. Though it's not targeted to quite the same audience as Kenn's first two educational books, he believes it will do well. "The book is aimed at anyone taking a first-year economics course in college, and it's easy enough for high schoolers to read. But my guess is that, like my other books, we'll sell most of the copies in bookstores to the curious adult market. It has nice blurbs, including one from former Governor Jerry Brown."

Kenn plans to continue focusing on non-fiction with a careful eye on the potential market for his new titles. "I think the market for *Algebra Unplugged* is ten times larger than the market for my electricity book. Two million students take their first algebra class each year. I've hardly tapped the potential sales for this book yet. My algebra book is selling faster now than the electricity book did after its first couple of years."

Besides promoting his existing titles, Kenn is working on his next book, *Calculus for Cats*. "Algebra is where I fell off the math track. Getting a D meant I couldn't become a doctor or an engineer. Algebra is where many people get stopped on the way to college, but if they do make it through algebra, then they can't figure out calculus."

It took Kenn three years to write *There Are No Electrons* and one year to edit it. *Algebra Unplugged* required only one year to write and a few months to edit. *Calculus for Cats* slowed Kenn down again. "Calculus was a little difficult for me to learn, for some reason, so that book moved slowly. But we'll have it done and released in 2000."

He thinks his next non-fiction title may be on music theory, but he's making no promises. "I like to find topics that interest me. I look for something I wouldn't mind learning about and then write a book on it. But I may take a break and rewrite one of my novels first. I may need to cleanse my muse's palate after *Calculus for Cats*."

Distributors and Bookstores

"You're somewhat at the mercy of the big players. You exist to a degree at their whim," Kenn says as he explains his company's relationship to companies such as Ingram and Baker & Taylor. "At the very first, before I was getting sales, the distributors didn't want to talk to me at all. I got orders directly from bookstores, and then Ingram decided to carry my book."

There Are No Electrons was picked up by the chain superstores after people came in and ordered copies. "The bookstores looked me up in Bowker's *Books in Print*," says Kenn. Because of demand, stores began to carry his books in stock. He keeps the demand strong by continually generating new reviews.

Kenn prefers to sell wholesale rather than retail. "My books aren't suitable for book tours. And I tried to get on about a dozen radio shows, but no one called me back. I can make much more money selling in volume anyway. It's cost effective, and I don't spend much time doing it."

Most of his sales go through two wholesalers, Baker & Taylor and Ingram. "I don't insist that orders be for case quantities, but they know how many of each title fit in a box. They usually order by the case."

After pulling each day's orders out of the fax machine, all Kenn does is stick on labels he has pre-printed with his wholesalers' addresses, and then places the boxes in his wife's car. "She works for her brother part-time, and she ships the boxes for me at work." The orders are shipped via UPS Ground.

The return rate on Kenn's books is only 1%, an unusually low rate compared to the national average. "The books come back scuffed so they can't be sold as new. I use those as review copies."

Copies are also sold through online bookstores such as Amazon.com. "*Algebra Unplugged* got as low as 2,000th on the list, *There Are No Electrons* stays at about 30,000th and *The Land of Debris and the Home of Alfredo* is at 500,000th."

Amazon.com allows authors and publishers to add a lot of information about their books to the online description, and Kenn takes advantage of this opportunity. "I save blurbs from all of the reviews I've gotten for the books on a disk in text format and send it to Amazon," Kenn says. "They put it online in about six weeks."

Though Kenn doesn't solicit direct sales from consumers, he provides ordering information for his two textbooks on the last pages of those books. He accepts credit cards, and says it was easy to get his merchant status. He pays no monthly fees, only a percentage of the amount charged.

Advice for the New Publisher

Kenn thinks new publishers should start off part-time. They need income from their current job until their books establish a solid sales record. "You don't have to work more than part-time hours to do a good job with your first book. But you shouldn't self-publish anything if you hate the idea of marketing, or if you think marketing is less noble than creating your manuscripts.

"Also, don't self-publish fiction unless you're willing to promote yourself as a mini-celebrity. It's just too difficult to get fiction reviewed if you're an unknown. If it's not reviewed, and you're not willing to be out there promoting it in person with book signings and interviews on the radio, how is anyone going to find out about your book? I'd consider e-publishing instead because the dollar risk is less. Maybe lightening will strike in a nice way."

Overall Kenn has enjoyed owning his own small press. "I didn't really know what would happen with the publishing. It's all been sort of a surprise. But I'm having fun and I plan to keep going until my books stop selling."

Chapter Fifteen

Switching to E-Books

Angela Adair-Hoy published her first book, *How to Be a Syndicated Newspaper Columnist*, in the traditional printed format, then converted it later to an electronic version to sell as an e-book from her web site, www.writersweekly.com. Sales were decent, though not world shaking.

Financial difficulties inspired her to write her next book. "I was unemployed for the first time in ten years. My refrigerator was broken, the pantry was bare, and I needed to find a way to feed my three children because their father wasn't paying his court-ordered child support. I was dating Richard (now my husband) at the time, but I never told him how bad things were. I was determined to make it on my own."

Angela says she wrote her second book in six hours. "I had received 10 e-mails that day asking about e-books. I thought, 'There really is a growing need here.' I sat down to write. By the next morning the book was complete."

Two years earlier Angela had started a monthly newsletter that listed current paying markets for freelance writers called the *Write Markets Report*, and a year later she had created a free e-magazine called *Writersweekly*. She promptly publicized her new book in the free e-magazine.

The response was immediate. "I sent out my weekly issue and offered my new book in it," Angela recalls. "Then I did a load of dishes, came back and sat down at my computer, and orders were flooding my mail box. Just bang, bang, bang."

That summer she received an e-mail from the owner of Booklocker.com. "He had heard about me and asked me to put my book, *How to Write, Publish and Sell E-books*, for sale on his site. I read his terms and they were extremely generous. Because he asked for non-exclusive rights I could keep selling my book through my web site. So I signed up. He put me on the home page because a lot of authors were coming there to learn about e-books. A couple of days after he put my book up, he had sold more than one hundred copies."

Buying Booklocker.com

Within months the owner of Booklocker.com approached Angela about buying the web site. "It had become too much for him. He needed somebody to buy it and take it to the next level. Richard and I snatched it up as fast as we could."

Angela continued with the same terms to authors as the previous owner had offered. "The authors earn 70% royalties. That makes people suspicious because we have the most generous terms in the book industry. They wondered what was in it for us. Few understood that we were determined to be the most author-friendly publisher online. We knew this would ultimately hurt our bottom line, but taking money from authors was not something we were willing to do. What surprised us in the end was that it helped our bottom line. Our reputation earned us a great deal of web site traffic and brought in more than 500 authors to Booklocker.

"We make our money from book sales, not from authors. That is the difference between Booklocker and vanity e-publishers. Vanity e-publishers make their profits from authors. They don't care if an author's book sells or not because they already have the author's money. We only make money on book sales, so it's in our best interest to help authors succeed in every way we can."

As an author, Angela wants to change the way publishing works. "If a new author goes with a traditional publisher, they're lucky to get 15% royalties. And if they're unknown and their book doesn't sell, the publisher won't allocate any marketing funds for the book. Then your book goes out of print, but you don't own the rights, so your book is dead. There's nothing you can do but write another book. If authors retain their electronic publishing rights, they are able to continue publishing their books online."

The tradition of paying authors only quarterly, or worse, anually, also irks Angela. In contrast, she points out that authors who self-publish and sell through their personal web sites can be paid as soon as they receive an order by credit card. If they choose to offer their books through an e-bookstore like Booklocker.com, they are paid monthly.

"As an author, I need a paycheck more often than every quarter," Angela says. "So we pay monthly. If we owe an author more than $10, then they get a check. What I keep in mind the entire time I'm doing business is how are the authors going to feel about this? What would I want if I were in their shoes?"

Angela is also concerned about the image of e-publishing. "A huge problem in electronic publishing right now is that because sites are so hungry for inventory, they will publish anything. This practice hurts the entire electronic publishing industry.

"Booklocker.com screens every incoming manuscript. After looking at so many books, I can tell who's a real author and who's looking to make a fast buck. If someone submits three novels that exceed three hundred pages, that's a series. If the first and last chapters are outstanding, these books probably have a home at Booklocker."

Other books get weeded out. "Once a woman submitted a three page e-book and I sent her a rejection letter. The next day she submitted a seven page e-book. I wrote her back and told her, 'Do not submit to Booklocker.com ever again.' She wasn't an author, she was an opportunist. But what scares me is that I know her 'e-books' are appearing on other sites."

Price Points for E-Books

Angela has experimented with different prices for her books. Not only has she discovered that prices above $15 hurt sales, but so do prices less than $8. "I can tell you that $8.95 is the magic number for e-books. I can offer a 50 page e-book by any author for $5 and nobody buys it. But if I offer a 50 page e-book at $8.95, everybody buys it, depending on the topic, of course."

As buying books electronically has become more common, Angela has seen prices rise. "It's a more accepted medium of delivery, and sales keep increasing. Every day sales exceed the day before. We are growing at an average rate of 40% a month in revenues."

Angela believes that people are willing to pay for the convenience of ordering from their own homes. "Consider that if you want to buy a book at the bookstore, you have to get dressed and get in your car, and pay for gas to drive to the bookstore. Buying e-books gives you instant delivery. You don't even have to get out of your chair, and you can have your book in seconds."

She has eliminated free books from Booklocker.com. "When we bought the web site it had several free e-books listed, and the first thing we did was take them down. First of all, most free e-books are promotional in nature. Second, we didn't want our starving authors to have their books compete with free e-books. And last, there are thousands of web sites now with free e-books available. That's fine if someone needs just anything to read, but the books we have aren't available somewhere else for free."

Starting an E-Magazine

Angela started her monthly magazine, *The Write Markets Report*, after she discovered the limitations of the standard printed guides for writers. "I bought *Writer's Market* hot from the printer and sent out a query letter. I got a letter back from an editor saying, 'You really need to update your database. That editor left here a year ago.' The book was the 1997 edition and it was only February!"

This experience made Angela realize that because the information for printed books is compiled months before the books are printed, she had an opportunity to provide more current information. "I decided I could find current paying markets for freelance writers and give them to those writers within two weeks of obtaining the information from editors."

Angela found the initial subscribers for her publication by offering free copies. "I sent out 1,000 free copies to people who had signed up at my new web site, and I asked people on several freelance writing lists to sign up. It really filled a need and it exploded."

The Write Markets Report is currently offered in electronic format only. "When it went from print to electronic, I lowered the price. We lost only three subscribers.

Subscribers are willing to pay for the e-magazine because it makes them money. "Each issue of *The Write Markets Report* features about 30 freelance markets, and they are all new. Nobody sees them before *The Write Markets Report* subscribers do. Most of them can land an assignment within a day or two of getting their issue, and that assignment more than pays for their annual subscription."

Marketing with a Free E-Magazine

Angela's free weekly e-magazine, *Writersweekly*, was originally published monthly just like *The Write Markets Report*. "I started it about a year after starting *The Write Markets Report* as a teaser issue to show people what they'd get if they subscribed to the *Report*. Plus I could put ads for my books in the free e-magazine. People want to subscribe because it delivers a whole list of current freelance jobs and more paying markets. Each issue, if printed, averages around 12 pages."

Being unemployed in the spring of 1999 inspired Angela to publish the free e-magazine weekly instead of monthly. With plenty of time and not a lot of money coming in the door, she hoped to increase the number of paying subscribers to the *Report* plus sell more of her books. "I could have kicked myself for not doing it sooner," Angela says. "My income quadrupled because people were getting my message four times a month instead of once."

The free e-magazine currently has over 30,000 subscribers. "Every Wednesday I send out an issue and every Wednesday I do $700 or $800 in sales of my own books. Probably 80% of the sales of my books come through the Writersweekly.com site and 20% through Booklocker.com." Angela's total sales for her own books total around $5,000 a month with an average price of $9 a book.

"With the *Writersweekly* e-magazine I know that when I write a new book I'm going to sell 300 or 400 copies right off the bat to the same people who have purchased every book I've written before." A fast writer, Angela plans to keep the new books coming. "All the books that I write have to help authors make more money. I want to help them no matter what their genre. This is their calling, and I want them to make a living at it."

Angela encourages all of the authors who put their books on Booklocker.com to start their own electronic magazine. "It's one of the things that is listed in the On-line Book Promotion E-kit we give to authors. It is by far the strongest marketing tool authors have for their books because they'll have a list of people wanting to hear from them on a regular basis. It's not just one contact with a potential buyer, but a weekly or monthly reminder saying, 'I'm still here. Have you bought my book yet?'"

When subscribers of her e-mags visit Angela's web site, they don't get a lot of glitz. "The site, while cosmetically somewhat appealing, appears to be an amateur website because I'm an amateur HTML person. We built a new, high tech and beautiful web site and put it up in the fall of 1999. Sales plummeted. We left the new site up for about three days, and then ripped that sucker down. It wasn't because of broken links or anything like that because we checked all the technical aspects of it. It was the design. We uploaded the old version and sales shot back up."

Angela believes she knows why the new site wasn't as successful. "The amateur part of my site gives people a feeling that they know me. They feel like they're dealing with a nice individual rather than a corporation. That's been a huge key to my success."

The personal touch also shows up in her e-mags. "I'll tell them about how my daughter, Ali, was in the emergency room Friday morning because she had a really bad nose bleed. Or when I lived in Texas, I would whine about how hot it is. Then Richard and I moved to Massachusetts for his job. It snows here every week so I put a blurb in about driving sideways down the street on the ice toward a school bus. People love that stuff. They feel like they are corresponding with a friend."

Angela's success with her e-mags led naturally to another book. "One of my best selling books is *How to Publish a Profitable E-Mag*, but I didn't use only my own story in that book. I obtained a list of large e-mags that had tens of thousands of subscribers. I sent these list owners questionnaires, then took the answers and compiled them to build my book out of the different topics these professionals had brought up. Readers get a whole medley of personal experiences."

Producing an E-Book

Most of the steps to producing a good e-book are the same as for any book. Angela writes her material, but she hires people to edit it and design the covers for her. "I hate editing, I absolutely despise it. It used to be a pet peeve of mine to find a typo on the front page of a newspaper, but now I'm much more understanding. After you've worked on something for 40, 50, or 60 hours, you don't see those typos anymore. They're ingrained in your memory, and they look fine."

Typos do slip into her e-mags. "There's the hurry factor," Angela explains. "I need to list a freelance job, and I've got to send my issue out right now. I don't have time to send it to the editor. It's a question of priorities. Information flows so fast these days that you just have to forgive those online typos."

Even with her books, Angela sometimes can't resist making a last minute change. "I sent my editor the final draft of a book. She went through it line by line and made all the corrections. She sent it back and said, 'Don't you dare touch it.'

"Of course I sat down and added a bunch of stuff, and didn't tell her what I did. The next day I sent out the book to all the people who had bought it for the pre-pub special price. I then received a few e-mails pointing out typos, so I sent it back to Valerie at ebookeditorial.com. She was not pleased with me because she is listed in the book as the editor."

Angela creates her copy in MS Word. "I format it just like a book with the page numbers and then I click file, print, print to PDF, and that's it." Then she uploads the book to her site and to Booklocker.com.

Though Angela doesn't require a cover for books to be on Booklocker.com, she does insist on individual covers for her own books. "The cover is what catches the buyer's eye. A cover is the way to let buyers know that this is a book, albeit in electronic format."

Though she freely admits she considers herself graphically impaired, Angela does have strong preferences for her covers. "I prefer photographs, not graphic designs. From my experience I can say that you have to be able to easily read the book's title. The font on the original cover has to be huge in order to shrink it down to 1 X 3 inches and still be able to read the title. There are a lot of e-book covers where you can't read what it says. Making the title large is the most important thing for an e-book."

Though Angela used to have a local printer do some print runs of 50 or so books for her customers who preferred hard copy over PDF, she doesn't plan to continue doing that. "We're going to go completely out of print with my books. If a buyer wants one, they'll either have to download it or order it on CD-ROM. I can make a CD-ROM a lot cheaper than I can print a book, and it's a lot less hassle."

Though Angela used to have an outside supplier burn her CD-ROMs for her, production has now shifted to her thirteen-year-old son, Zach. "He's started his own company, Bookburners.com. He's going to be strictly burning e-books onto CD-ROMs for authors. He charges authors $3 to $5 per CD depending on how many they order."

By offering her books on CD-ROMs, Angela is able to sell her books through the large online bookstores. "I've sold dozens of copies of the CD-ROMs through Amazon. The customer gets it with a cute little cover. It comes with three files: a read me file that's just text to tell them how to access and read their book, the Adobe Acrobat reader, the most recent version which automatically installs itself on their computer, and the e-book itself."

Watching for Copyright Infringement

"I've found my copyrighted material on other web sites," Angela says. She takes a hard line approach to people who steal her words. "I've shut down two web sites; it's not too hard to do. You call the ISP and say they have copyrighted material on their server that belongs to you. Send them proof that it is your material and that it is copyrighted, and demand they take it down. ISPs will do as you ask because at the moment they become aware that their server harbors illegal material, they become legally liable as well."

Angela is very up front about her attitude. "My blurb that we prosecute for copyright infringement, no exceptions, is everywhere. We have to be aggressive and consistent to protect ourselves and our authors."

Although she has experienced theft of material from her web site and e-mags, Angela hasn't had a problem with anyone taking content from an e-book and republishing it. "I did have one gentleman call and say he wanted to put my e-books on his web site, their entire contents, but it would be for members only, for people who subscribe to his web site. And in exchange, he would give me free advertising.

"I said, 'Excuse me?' And he said, 'It's a members only area on my web site, so even if I put it up, you would never know.' And I told him, 'I've got a lot of friends in the industry. As soon as someone sees you doing that and lets me know, I will put you out of business without hesitation.'"

Technological advances are making it easier to protect material. "We utilize the highest security we can. Adobe came out with an upgrade to version 4.0, and in their words, the only way someone will be able to take an e-book off their computer will be to remove the hard drive. The book file will be protected so it cannot be attached to an e-mail or uploaded."

Refunds on E-Books

Angela includes a statement on receipts that says all sales are final, but sometimes she will be a bit flexible. "If we receive word from a buyer that they are not happy with the purchase because they thought the book would have different content or it didn't include the information they were looking for on a particular topic, then I'll refund their money."

Refunds aren't given with no questions asked, however. "The reason we have that statement on our receipt is that we have experienced buyers coming in and purchasing 10 e-books at a time. They receive them and within seconds they send us an e-mail saying 'Oh, we can't open any of these' or 'These are terrible books.' It's obvious they haven't had time to even open the books, much less read them. They are trying to shoplift electronically, and I say, 'Sorry, no refund.'"

Angela doesn't pussyfoot around when she explains that no refunds will be made to people she feels are trying to steal. "One woman responded to every single e-book we delivered within seconds that she couldn't read them and please issue a refund. I wrote her back and said, 'It's people like you that make writers starving artists. These authors need to feed their families just like you need to feed yours.' I copied the authors on the e-mail, and refused to issue the woman a refund."

The Future of E-Books

Angela believes e-books are the wave of the future. "Just like television dominated the radio and the automobile replaced the horse and buggy, e-books are going to dominate the publishing industry. People aren't going to like it at first, but they're going to get used to it just like every other advancement in technology. I think in the next 5-10 years you will be able to find any book you want as an e-book, but you're going to have to hunt for the print version of it."

Publishers have offered to buy the rights to Angela's e-book *How to Write, Publish and Sell E-books* so they can produce it in a printed version. "I was offered two contracts for this book. Both publishers offered me a $5,000 advance and they wanted all the rights. I said no. I can make that much in a month all by myself."

Another of Angela's e-books made it into print as a selection of the Doubleday and Literary Book Club and was then picked up by St. Martin's Press. "M.J. Rose, a famous e-author, called me one day. She said she had a book idea and I was the perfect person to write it with her. I said yes because of her outstanding reputation and her drive. I knew we were a perfect match to co-author a book on electronic publishing. I knew parts of the industry she didn't know, and she knew parts I didn't know."

Their co-authored book, *The Secrets of Our Success: How to Publish and Promote Online*, came out as an e-book in the fall of 1999, and the book club rights and print rights sold at auction in early 2000. "We were adamant about not selling the electronic rights to this book, and we succeeded in the end," Angela says.

Advice for the Would-Be Electronic Publisher

Angela thinks that anyone with perseverance and desire can succeed in electronic publishing. "If I can do it, anybody can. I believe that every curve ball that comes my way just makes me stronger. It makes me work harder and have a better sense of humor about things."

Certain types of books sell better than others through her Booklocker.com site. "If someone hasn't written their book yet, and they're looking for the best one to earn money, they need to write a non-fiction how-to-make-money book. Not a garbage book, a multi-level marketing, income opportunity book, but a legitimate how to start your own business type of book. These books are the best sellers."

However, Angela has seen a real increase in the sales of other types of books, including fiction. "When Richard and I first bought Booklocker.com, fiction wasn't selling. People just weren't buying electronic fiction, but then around Christmas time in 1999, fiction sales exploded."

Angela keeps learning about new topics that sell well. "I had the best selling book on Booklocker.com for months when Jill Henry came out of nowhere and knocked me off the number one spot. I was happy for her, but I was shocked because her book is *Gifts from the Heart of the Home: Edible Gifts for All Occasions*. I know non-fiction books sell better than fiction, but edible gifts? There's a whole market out there that even I'm not aware of. People love arts and crafts, and they love learning how to make their own stuff."

So whatever books authors want to write, Angela thinks they should give electronic publishing a chance. They won't risk a lot of money, but they just might sell a lot of books. "Many authors won't e-publish because of their fears about security," she says. "First, I tell them to put plenty of ads for all of their products and services at the end of each of their electronic books. Then if someone gets a bootlegged copy of your e-book and they like it enough, they'll come back and buy something else from you.

"Second, I tell them that if I hadn't e-published because of fear of copyright infringement, I would be out of business. It's like being afraid of getting in a car accident so you never go to the grocery store. Well, then you starve. To make money, you've got to put your book out there."

Although Angela can see how having a book published by a large publisher would make any author feel great, she keeps practical concerns at the top of her list. "I've always said that my pocketbook has to be bigger than my vanity. I could have sold the rights to my book, and right now I could drive to the Barnes and Noble store in Salem, New Hampshire, and see my book on the shelf, but that doesn't feed my kids. I make a lot more money self-publishing e-books than I could through a traditional publisher."

Afterword

The self-publishers profiled in *Make Money Self-Publishing* demonstrate that a wide variety of people can successfully start and run small publishing companies. Some people such as Kenn Amdahl prefer to promote their books instead of themselves while others, for example M.J. Rose or Gordon Miller, are happy to put themselves in the public eye. Each publisher has selected the promotional methods that best suit their personalities.

They've found success publishing books that cover a range of topics. From cookbooks to job advice, regional guides to mysteries and erotic literary fiction, the market for self-published books is wide open. The secrets to success pertain more to the quality of the books and a persistence in marketing them as opposed to a self-publisher who is lucky at picking a hot topic.

Although these publishers have proven that there are many profitable ways to sell self-published books, their stories reveal common threads that can guide you as you strive to sell a sufficient quantity of books quickly enough to earn a decent living as a self-publisher.

Top Ten Tips to Make Money Self-Publishing

1) Publish at least three titles. Although the occasional publisher such as Barbara Hudgins can make a living on the sales of just one title, having multiple titles makes it much easier. Sometimes sales for a particular title slow down over time, as Sue and Rich Freeman experienced with their regional guides. Sometimes a book reaches the end of its life as Diane Pfeiffer discovered with one of her titles, *Stick with Your Pan*. Sometimes a book continues to sell well, but just not in large enough numbers to support you by itself. Wille Ripple's first book, *Halloween School Parties...What Do I Do?*®, continued to sell well its second and third year, but it was the addition of the second book in her series that swung her net income into the comfortable five digits.

You may think you have only one book in you, but you'll probably be surprised by the new book ideas that pop up after your first book is published. The key is to keep your mind and heart open to the possibility of another book, and realize that it may take more than one title if you want publishing to completely support you.

2) Develop a series or specialize in one category of books.
Whether you are writing fiction or how-to books, buyers like to buy books in a series. Let each of your books sell the others by establishing some sort of connection. Whether you give them a common name like Peter Kent did with his Poor Richard series of computer books, publish books with continuing characters like Connie Shelton with her mysteries, or stick with a certain category of books like Virginia and Robert Hoffman with their wine related cookbooks, series make it far easier to sell your books.

Sometimes you won't know at the beginning what types of books will become your specialty. It's fine to experiment as long as you arrange your financial situation properly. Give yourself time to find your niche by having other sources of income. Then remember to focus. In the long term you will do better financially if you publish related books.

3) Focus on books that are evergreen.
Textbooks and cookbooks can sell for years before they have to be rewritten. Cherie Thurston's books for middle school students age grace-

fully because teaching English requires the same materials from year to year. Guidebooks and technology books, however, will require you to spend a substantial amount of time writing revisions. New editions must be created regularly. This can become a problem because it's hard to grow a company and increase your profit potential if you have to devote your time to revising old books instead of writing new ones.

4) If your titles have a limited shelf life, then work with an exclusive distributor. If you deal with seasonal books like Willie Ripple does, or time sensitive topics with information that becomes dated quickly like Peter Kent, then you've got to have the ability to get quantities of your books into the bookstores relatively fast. An effective exclusive distributor has the power to do this, though it's not always easy to get your books accepted by a reputable distributor. You will also have to price your books to allow for the larger distributor cut.

5) Participate in online bookstores. Book sales through online stores continue to grow incredibly fast. You need to make sure Amazon.com, BarnesandNoble.com, and Borders.com have your best reviews posted, color graphics of your cover, and comments from you as the publisher and author. You also need to actively encourage enthusiastic readers to post positive reviews.

Online bookstores have effectively erased one of the two biggest problems small presses have faced: lack of distribution. Internet bookstores have made it possible for self-publishers to offer their books nationwide even when local bookstores don't carry their titles. As long as publishers successfully publicize their books, readers will be able to buy them no matter where they live.

It's vital that your books be as close to instantly available online as possible. Buyers want to see your title in stock and ready to ship. The difference between 4-6 weeks availability and 24 hours for your titles can be a 500% increase in monthly sales through Amazon.com. Their Advantage program sells a lot of small press books, and it's easy to join by going to their site.

Participation in the Advantage program requires giving Amazon.com a 55% discount, but you can afford to offer online bookstores larger discounts than you can to brick and mortar bookstores. Why? There are two reasons. First, the risk of damaged returns is minimized. Few shoppers have a chance to give your books that not-so-charming shop worn look.

Second, your percentage of returned books will be reduced. Instead of sending your titles to dozens of bookstores, either directly or through a wholesaler, you usually send books to one location for each online bookstore. They order what they need to fill their anticipated quantity of sales for your titles, maybe a few weeks' worth, and rarely send you returns. You avoid wasting your time and money shipping out books only to have them show up on your doorstep six months later.

The reality is that selling online is a more cost efficient way to sell books. Your larger discounts can be compensated by your lower selling costs as well as by an increased volume of sales. You'll likely make more money despite the larger discount required to get the coveted 24 hour shipping status.

6) Explore e-books. As e-books become more accepted, you'll lose sales if your books aren't available in electronic format. You can sign up with non-exclusive sites e-bookstores so you can offer your titles through your own web site as well as through the e-bookstores, or you can sign up with an exclusive e-bookstore. You may decide to skip offering your books in printed format like Angela Adair-Hoy did. Focusing on e-books allows small publishers to avoid the costs of inventory and the risk of printing too many copies of a particular book.

7) Educate yourself. You should join publisher associations, go to publishing conferences, read publishing newsletters and magazines, and/or participate in a publisher list serv. The resources for self-publishers abound, and many of them are free or low cost. Learn about the competition as well as about the publishing business. Try out your ideas before you commit to publishing a book.

Virginia and Robert Hoffman attended publishing conferences and joined associations before they published their first cookbook. Rich and Sue Freeman did research at the library. Barbara Hudgins wrote about travel as a columnist before she compiled her pieces into her first book. And M.J. Rose offered her book online as a way to gauge demand.

8) Look for other ways to sell your books. Think beyond the idea of selling books through bookstores. Would some company like to use your book as a premium? Have you thought about selling books at a holiday show? Through gift stores? As a fund raiser for a charity instead of chocolate bars or magazine subscriptions? Should you start your own e-newsletter? Would a catalog company be interested in carrying one of your titles? Always keep your mind open to new or different ways to sell your books.

Bonnie Makowski-Probart exchanges columns for ad space, Gayle Mitchell offers gambling tip cards through Bottom Line PERSONAL magazine, and Barbara Hudgins speaks to newcomers groups. Think about alternative ways to market your books. Those extra sales can mean the difference between a small publishing income and an income large enough to allow you to quit your day job.

9) Sell your rights to another publisher. Even if all you want is to be a publisher, the day will come when you or your heirs will wish to sell your publishing business. Have you developed a coherent list of books that would be desirable to another publisher? Have you built up a valuable mailing list of direct customers or retail stores who buy from you regularly? Have you invested the money and promotional time to keep your backlist titles selling well?

Connie Shelton's company attracted buyout interest because her press had developed a good reputation in the mystery category. Diane Pfeiffer bought another publisher's list of titles because that publisher had penetrated the big box retailer market. If you develop a particular strength with your list of titles, you'll increase your company's value.

If you want to sell rights to just one title, you'll need to develop a buzz around your book in a manner similar to what Gordon Miller or M.J. Rose did. To get impressive results fast enough to catch the attention of a big publisher, you'll need to work hard with a concentrated burst of effort. Become a big fish in a small pond by focusing your promotional efforts regionally, online, or in some other area that you identify as suitable for your book.

10) Think big. Try to get a national columnist or TV personality to review your book. Send your galleys to the appropriate book clubs. Contact possible premium buyers. Offer your titles to a company such as Reading's Fun.

Although it would be a gamble for you to concentrate only on long shot proposals to the exclusion of more mundane ways of selling books, even a conservative self-publisher should invest a portion of available time and energy trying for the big score. While typical day-to-day sales pay the regular bills, one big hit could be the financial ticket that puts you on the train to full-time self-publishing. Big premium sales have been the key to Diane Pfeiffer's success as a publisher.

Additional Information

Additional information to help you succeed as a self-publisher is provided in the following appendices. Whether you want to contact a company mentioned by one of the profiled self-publishers, read a recommended book, join an association or list serv, or research online marketing opportunities, you'll find the necessary names, phone numbers, and addresses in the appropriate appendix. For updates, visit the *Make Money Self-Publishing* web site at www.MakeMoneySelfPublishing.com.

Appendix A - Profiled Publishing Companies

Angela Adair-Hoy
www.writersweekly.com
www.booklocker.com
aadair@writersweekly.com
aadair@booklocker.com
Fax: 207-262-5544

Kenn Amdahl
Clearwater Publishing Co. Inc.
P.O. Box 778
Broomfield, CO 80038-0778
Phone: 303-436-1982
Fax: 303-465-2741
www.clearwaterpublishing.com

Rich and Sue Freeman
Footprint Press
P.O. Box 645
Fishers, NY 14453
Phone: 716-421-9383
E-mail: rich@footprintpress.com
www.footprintpress.com

Virginia and Robert Hoffman
The Hoffman Press
P.O. Box 2868
Santa Rosa, CA 95405
Fax: 707-538-7371
www.foodandwinecookbooks.com

Barbara Hudgins
The Woodmont Press
Box 108
Green Village, NJ 07935
908-647-6039
E-mail: njdaytrips@aol.com
www.woodmontpress.com
www.njdaytrips.com

Peter Kent
Top Floor Publishing
8790 W. Colfax, Ste. 107
Lakewood, CO 80215
Phone: 303-205-9861
www.TopFloor.com

Bonnie Markowski-Probart
K & B Products
P.O. Box 1502, PMB 214
Red Bluff, CA 96080
E-mail: BRMP@aol.com
www.TheCompletePet.com

Gayle Mitchell
Casino Players Workshop & Seminars
4001 E. Bell Rd. #114-270
Phoenix, AZ 85032
Orders: 888-208-7117
E-mail: gmitchell@easycasinogambling.com
www.easycasinogambling.com

Diane Pfeiffer
Strawberry Patch
PO Box 52404
Atlanta, GA 30355-0404
E-mail: DiPfeifer@aol.com
www.strawberrypatch.net

Willie Ripple
Oakbrook Publishing House
P.O. Box 2463
Littleton, CO 80161-2463
Phone: 303-738-1733
Fax: 303-797-1995
E-mail: Oakbrook@whatdoidobooks.com
www.whatdoidobooks.com

MJ Rose
Agent, Loretta Barretta Books: 212-242-3420
E-mail: MJRoseAuthor@aol.com

Connie Shelton
Columbine Publishing Group
P.O. Box 456
Angel Fire, NM 87710
Publishing consultation services available - ask for brochure
that describes services and fees
E-mail: mystery@afweb.com

Cheri Thurston
Cottonwood Press, Inc.
305 West Magnolia, Suite 398
Fort Collins, CO 80521
Orders: 800-864-4297
Phone: 970-204-0715
E-mail: cottonwood@cottonwoodpress.com
www.cottonwoodpress.com

Appendix B - Publisher & Writer Associations

Arizona Book Publishing Association
957 E. Guadalupe Rd., Box 20
Tempe, AZ 85283
Phone: 602-274-6264

Association of Authors and Publishers
PO Box 35038
Houston, TX 77235-5038
www.authorsandpublishers.org

Audio Publishers Association
627 Aviation Way
Manhattan Beach, CA 90266
Phone: 310-372-0546
Fax: 310-374-3342
E-mail: apaonline@aol.com

Austin Writers' League
1501 W. Fifth St., Ste. E-2
Austin, TX 78703
www.writersleague.org

Bay Area Independent Publishers
P.O. Box E
Corte Madera, CA 94976
Phone: 415-257-8275
www.baipa.org

Book Publishers Northwest
PO Box 99642
Seattle, WA 98199
Phone: 425-885-3173

Book Publishers of Texas
P.O. Box 831495
Richardson, TX 75083-1495
Phone: 972-671-0002
www.authorlink.com/bpt.html

Catholic Book Publishers Association, Inc.
2 Park Avenue
Manhasset, New York 11030
E-mail: cbpa3@aol.com

Colorado Independent Publishers Association (CIPA)
P.O. Box 4008
Boulder, CO 80306
Phone: 303-629-3080
www.cipabooks.com

Community Writers Association
P.O. Box 312
Providence, RI 02901-0312
www.communitywriters.org

Connecticut Authors & Publishers Association
PO Box 715
Avon, CT 06001
Phone: 203-729-5335
Fax: 860-676-0759
E-mail: CAA@marketingdirections.com

Florida Publishers Association
PO Box 430
Highland City, FL 33846-0430
Phone: 941-647-5951
E-mail: FPAbooks@aol.com
www.flbookpub.org

Georgia Independent Publishers Association
P.O. Box 108
Redan, GA 30074-0108
Phone: 770-808-0793

Houston Council of Writers
P.O. 441381
Houston, TX 77244-1381

Independent Publishers Association Canada
PO Box 22184
Calgary, Alberta T2P 4J1, Canada

Independent Publishers Guild
P.O. Box 93
Royston SG8 5GH
England
Phone: 01763 247014
Fax: 01763 246293
E-mail: info@ipg.uk.com
www.ipg.uk.com

Independent Publishers for Christ
P.O. Box 280349
Lakewood, CO 80228

Independent Publishers of New England
P.O. Box 1164
Northampton, MA 01061

Marin Small Publishers Association
(changed to Bay Area Independent Publishers)

Mid-America Publishers Association
Chapter of Publishers Marketing Association
Phone: 310-372-2732

MidAtlantic Publishers Association
c/o Summit Crossroads Press
126 Camp Harmison Dr.
Berkeley Springs, WV 25411
E-mail: SumCross@aol.com

Midwest Independent Publishers Association
P.O. Box 581432
Minneapolis, MN 55458-1432
Phone: 651-917-0021

Multicultural Publishing & Education Council
177 South Kihei Rd.
Kihei, Maui, HI 96753
E-mail: mpec@aol.com
www.mpec.org

National Writers Association
3140 S. Peoria #295
Aurora, CO 80014

New Age Publishers and Retailing Alliance
P.O. Box 9
109 North Beach Rd.
Eastsound, WA 98245
Phone: 360-376-2702

New Editions International, Ltd.
P.O. Box 2578
Sedona, AZ 86339
Phone: 520-282-9574
Fax: 520-282-9730
E-mail: newedit@sedona.net

New Mexico Book Association
P.O. Box 1285
Santa Fe, NM 87504
www.nmbook.org

Northwest Assocation of Book Publishers
P.O. Box 3786
Wilsonville, OR 97070-3786

Organization of Book Publishers of Ontario
Ste. 301
720 Batherst St.
Toronto, Ontario M5S 2R4
Phone: 416-536-7584

Publishers Association of the South
4412 Fletcher St.
Panama City, FL 32405-1017
Phone: 850-914-0766
Fax: 850-769-4348
E-mail: info@pubsouth.org
www.pubsouth.org

Publishers Association of the West
P.O. Box 19013
Boulder, CO 80308
Phone: 303-499-9540
www.rmbpa.com

Publishers Marketing Association
627 Aviation Way
Manhattan Beach, CA 90266
Phone: 310-372-2732
E-mail: info@pma-online.org
www.pma-online.org

Rocky Mountain Book Publisher Association
(changed to Publishers Association of the West)

Rocky Mountain Fiction Writers
P.O. Box 260244
Denver, CO 80226-0244
Phone: 303-331-2608
www.rmfw.org

Sacramento Publishers Association
P.O. Box 60954
Sacramento, CA 95860

San Diego Publishers Alliance
c/o Bob Goodman
Silvercat
4070 Goldfinch St., Ste CP.O. Box 1306
San Diego, CA 92103
Phone: 619-299-6774

Sisters in Crime
P.O. Box 442124
Lawrence, KS 66044
Phone: 785-842-1325
Fax: 785-842-1034
E-mail: sistersincrime@juno.com
www.sistersincrime.org

Small Publishers Association of North America
P.O. Box 1306
425 Cedar Street
Buena Vista, CO 81211-1306
Phone: 719-395-4790
SPAN@SPANnet.org
www.SPANnet.org

Small Publishers , Artists & Writers Network
P.O. Box 2653
Ventura, CA 93002-2653
Phone: 805-643-2403

Southern Independent Publishers Association
12610 Hwy. 90 West
Grand Bay, AL 36541
Phone: 334-865-1500
Fax: 334-865-6252
E-mail: SIPSAL@juno.com
www.laughingowl.com/sips.htm

Upper Peninsula Publishers and Authors Association
Rt 1 Box 52
Cooks, MI 49817

Appendix C - List Servs

List servs are online discussion groups that discuss various topics. The two largest publisher list servs are PUBLISH-L and Publisher's Forum. PUBLISH-L is generally well mannered and sticks to how-to questions. Publisher's Forum can sometimes be a bit raucous because its discussion also includes the philosophy of publishing, based sometimes on strongly held personal beliefs. To subscribe to these lists go to:

http://pub-forum.webjump.com

www.guestfinder.com/publishlist.htm

Amazon-Affiliates' discussion list focuses on marketing and profit improvement for online bookstores. Open to anyone who sells or wants to sell books online. Subscription details are at

http://st3.yahoo.net/onlinemarketing/amazon.html

If you want support as a writer, the Association of Authors and Publishers has started a discussion group. Click on "Join Our E-mail Community" on their homepage at:

www.authorsandpublishers.org

Another discussion group for writers can be found in the "CafeLit" at:

www.CommunityWriters.org

Appendix D -
Companies and Service
Providers

Books in Print

R. R. Bowker
121 Chanlon Road
New Providence, NJ 07974
Phone: 908-665-6770
Fax: 908-665-2895
www.bowker.com

Book Cover Designer

Bob Schaum of Bookends
1920 13th St., Ste. B
Boulder, CO 80302
Phone: 303-443-8277

Bobbi Shupe of EPI Puffen & Company
P.O. 36242
Denver, CO 50236
Phone: 303-985-3390

Booklets

Paulette Ensign
TPI
www.tipsbooklet.com

Credit Cards/Web Site Orders

CCNow
www.CCNow.com

Distributors and Wholesalers

Baker & Taylor
P.O. Box 8888
Momence IL 60954
Phone: 908-722-8000
www.btol.com

Bookazine Company, Inc.
75 Hook Rd.
Bayonne, NJ 07002
Phone: 201-339-7777
www.bookazine.com

Independent Publishing Group (IPG)
814 N. Franklin St.
Chicago, IL 60610
Phone: 312-337-0747
Fax: 312-337-5985
www.ipgbook.com

Ingram Book Company
Publishers Relations Department
One Ingram Blvd.
P.O. Box 3006
La Vergne, TN 37086-3629
E-mail: pubrel@ingrambook.com
www.ingrambookgroup.com/Pub_Info/newpubinfo/

Koen Book Distributors
10 Twosome Dr.
P.O. Box 600
Moorestown, NJ 08057
Phone: 800-257-8481
Fax: 800-225-3840
www.koen.com

Midpoint Trade Books
27 W. 20th St., #1102
New York, NY 10011-3707
Phone: 212-727-0190
E-mail: midpointny@aol.com
www.midpointtrade.com

Mother Pickle Distributing
1 30 Kincardine Rd. Unit 3
Walkerton, ON NOG 2VO, Canada
c/o Norman G. Jensen Inc.
1908 Dove St.
Port Huron, MI 48060, USA
Phone: 519-881-0051
Fax: 519-881-0057
www.motherpickle.on.ca

Quality Books Inc.
1003 W. Pines Road
Oregon, IL 61061-9680
Phone: 815-732-4450
Fax: 815-732-4499

the distributors
702 S. Michigan
South Bend, IN 46601
Phone: 219-232-8500

Unique
5010 Kemper Ave.
St. Louis, MO 63139
Phone: 800-533-5446

Valentine Publishing Group
P.O. Box 902582
Palmdale, CA 93590-2582
www.vpg.net

Editor

Ebookeditorial.com
700 Ken Pratt Blvd., Ste. #264-353
Longmont, CO 80501
Fax: 303-684-9269
E-mail: editor@ebookeditorial.com

Fulfillment Service

Book Clearing House
46 Purdy Street
Harrison, NY 10528
Phone: 914-835-0015
www.book-clearing-house.com

Publishers Storage & Shipping Corp. (MA)
46 Development Rd.
Fitchburg, MA 01420
Phone: 978-345-2121
Fax: 978-348-1233

Publishers Storage & Shipping Corp. (MI)
660 S. Mansfield
Ypsilanti, MI 48197
Phone: 734-487-9720
Fax: 734-487-1890

Publishers Storage & Shipping Corp. (NJ)
51 Stiles Lane
Pine Brook, NJ 07058-9535
Phone: 973-244-1313
Fax: 973-244-9111

Rayve Productions
P.O. Box 726
Windsor, CA 95492
Phone: 707-836-6200
Fax: 707-838-2220
E-mail: Rayve@SPANnet.org

Magazines for Giveaway Offers

Bottom Line Personal Magazine
P.O. Box 58446
Boulder, CO 80322-8446
Phone: 800-274-5611
Fax: 303-604-7455
www.bottomlinepersonal.com

Freebies Magazine
For sample copy send $3.00 to Freebies Publishing
P.O. Box 310
Carpinteria, CA 93014-0310
Phone: 805-566-1225
Fax:805-566-0305

Printers

Bang
1473 Hwy. 18 East
P.O. Box 587
Brainerd, MN 56401
Phone:1-800-328-0450
Fax: 218-829-7145

Data Reproductions
4545 Glenmeade Lane
Auburn Hilss, MI 48326
Phone: 248-371-3700 or 800-242-3114
Fax: 248-371-3701
www.datarepro@wwnet.net

Central Plains Book Manufacturing (run by former Gilliland employees)
22234 C Street, Strother Field
Winfield, KS 67156
Phone: 877-278-2726
Fax: 316-221-4762
www.centralplainsbook.com

KNI
1261 S. State College Parkway
Anaheim, CA 92806
Phone: 800-886-7301
E-mail: knimb@aol.com

Kendall Printing
3331 W. 29th St.
Greeley, CO 80631
Phone: 970-330-8895

McNaughton & Gunn, Inc.
960 Woodland Dr.
Saline, MI 48176
Phone: 734-429-5411
Fax: 1-800-677-2665
www.bookprinters.com

Thomson-Shore
7300 W. Joy Rd.
Dexter, MI 48130-9701
Phone: 734-426-3939
Fax: 734-426-6219 or 800-706-4545

United Graphics
2916 Marshall Ave.
P.O. Box 559
Mattoon, IL 61938
Phone: 217-235-7161
Fax: 217-234-6274

Specialty Sales

Reading's Fun (also called Books Are Fun)
Reader's Digest Books
123 N. Main St.
Fairfield, IA 52556
www.booksarefun.com

Review Publications

Booklist
Up Front, Advance Reviews
50 E. Huron St.
Chicago, IL 60611
Phone: 312-944-6780
Fax: 312-337-6787

Kirkus Reviews
Library Advance Information Service
200 Park Avenue South, Ste. 1118
New York, NY 10003
Phone: 212-777-4554
Fax: 212-979-1352

Library Journal
Book Review Editor
245 W. 17th St.
New York, NY 10011
Phone: 212-463-6819
Fax: 212-463-6734

Publishers Weekly
Forecasts
245 W. 17th St.
New York, New York 10011
Phone: 212-463-6758
Fax: 212-463-6631

Appendix E - Useful Web Sites

Book Signings

Many sites list upcoming book signings. Some also notify media about posted events. Try:
www.publishersweekly.com/highway/
www.NetRead.com/calendar

If you want to set up book signings, both Barnes and Noble and Borders have a store locator button on their home page that allows you to type in a zip code and get the nearest stores, the next nearest stores, continuing until you have as many leads as you want.
www.BarnesandNoble.com
www.Borders.com

Copyright

If you want to download the Form TX to register your copyright, you'll need a PDF reader such as Adobe Acrobat. This PDF reader is available free at www.adobe.com. The Form TX is available at www.loc.gov/copyright/forms/formtxi.pdf.
Lots of information on copyright is available at:
www.execpc.com/~mbr/bookwatch/writepubl.

If you want help getting paid royalties for your material published on the world wide web, visit Copyright Clearance Center at:
www.copyright.com

Dictionaries and Research

Lists of online dictionaries, encyclopedias, thesaurus, zip code datebases and more reside at:
www.yourdictionary.com
www.refdesk.com

Galleys

For pre-publicity galleys, check out prices and options at:

www.craneduplicating.com

General

The Midwest Book Review site is almost overwhelming in its level of detail. You should go first to the "Advice for Publishers" section at:
www.execpc.com/~mbr/bookwatch/writepub

Dan Poynter's site is another treasure trove of publisher information You can also order mailing lists at:
www.ParaPub.com

The main publishing magazine, *Publishers Weekly*, has a web site at:
www.publishersweekly.com

John Kremer, one of the marketing gurus of self-publishing can be found at:
www.bookmarket.com/selfpublish.html

Genre

If you are writing fiction, numerous sites are devoted to the various genres. These sites can help you do market research and get publicity for your books. Some to try:

www.themysteryreader.com
www.theromancereader.com
www.romancejournal.com
www.writerspace.com

Legal

Articles about a variety of topics are available at these two sites.

www.ivanhoffman.com
www.publaw.com

Libraries

Tom Person offers an old-fashioned paper newsletter for publishers full of handy tips and recommendations, but he also provides a list of almost 200 libraries with large purchasing budgets at his web site. If you plan on doing library solicitations, this list is a good start at:

www.laughingbear.com/library.html

Media Listings

Newspapers and magazines are seachable, plus links are provided at:

www.gebbieinc.com

Online Bookstores

The biggie of them all is Amazon.com. Finding their instructions for publishers interested in selling their books through Amazon.com can be confusing. Try:
www.amazon.com/exec/obidos/subst/partners/direct/direct-application.html

To find out who is selling your book online and for what price, check at:
www.bestbookbuys.com

Prices

A number of sites provide sample prices for desktop services such as page layout, graphic design, web design, proofreading, editing, illustration, and logo design. Sometimes you'll only find teasers, but just a little information may be enough to give you a starting point. Try:
www.brennerbooks.com
www.tiac.net/users/freelanc/

Publicity

To find out special event dates to hook to your book in a press release, visit:
www.celebratetoday.com

If you want to hire someone to fax out your press release, investigate:
www.imediafax.com
www.book-publicity.com

If you want to hire someone to write press releases, do a media blitz for just one city or the entire nation, or set up radio spots for you, look at:
www.talion.com

For a lot of good advice on publicity, visit MarciaYudkin's siteto look at an assortment of good articles:
www.yudkin.com

R.R. Bowker

R.R. Bowker produces Books In Print and Forthcoming Books in Print. You can register as a publisher at:
www.bowker.com/titleforms/home/index.html

To make updates or changes visit:
www.booksinprint.com

Selling Rights to Books

The Internet functions best when it enables people to market their goods to a widespread pool of buyers. Whereas publishers have historically relied on a network of agents and sub-agents to sell a variety of subsidiary rights, the future looks different. Check out one of the first online middlemen at:
www.rightsworld.com

Web Site

If you want help designing and hosting a web site, try:
www.bookzone.com
www.websightsolutions.com

If you want to sell books through your web site without having to handle the transactions, become an Amazon.com Associate. You can find out how to sign up and how to link to Amazon.com by visiting their homepage and clicking on the button that says Associates.

To research what links from other sites bring viewers to your site's pages, go to Altavista.com and type, Link:Your web site address, into the search box.

If you want to research companies to host your web site, visit:

www.webhostdir.com

Writer's Sites

You may want to attend conferences as a speaker, vendor, or student. For ideas visit:

www.shawguides.com

If you want the online company of other writers plus interesting articles about writing and publishing, visit:

www.inkspot.com

www.novalearn.com

Appendix F - Useful E-Zines

Book Marketing Tip of the Week
John Kremer provides ideas on marketing books in this handy
weekly bulletin. Subscribe at:
     www.bookmarket.com

Bright Ideas!
Cathy Stucker provides a visibility and marketing strategy
every week. Subscribe at:
     www.idealady.com/bright.htm

Foreword Magazine
For news of the independent publishing world send an e-mail
message with "subscribe forewordyourfirstnameyourlastname"
to:
     lists@brightbridge.net

Freelance $uccess
Although the newsletter costs money, you can check their
archive of sample articles before you pony up. Check it out at:
     www.freelancesuccess.com

!Get Published!
More news of the publishing world. To subscribe send a blank
e-mail to:
     getpub-subscribe@getpub.com

Painted Rock
A free newsletter that focus on genre fiction. To sign up, go to:
     www.paintedrock.com

Poor Richard's Website News

Peter Kent offers ideas on how to build, maintain, and promote your web site in this newsletter. Subscribe at:

www.poorrichard.com

PubLaw Update

Lloyd L. Rich, a lawyer who specializes in publishing, offers a free publishing law newsletter. Subscribe at:

www.publaw.com

Websight Insight

Check out an archive of articles on using web sites to promote your business and subscribe to new issues at:

www.websightsolutions.com/insight

Writers Weekly

Angela Adair-Hoy provides listings of markets each week. Some opportunities may be ideal for you as vehicles to publicize your book. To subscribe send an a-mail to:

writemarkets-subscribe@onelist.com

Appendix G - Recommended Books

General

Complete Guide to Self-Publishing
Tom and Marilyn Ross

Publishing for Profit
Thomas Woll

The Self-Publishing Manual
Dan Poynter

Publicity

1001 Ways to Sell Your Book
John Kremer

6 Steps to Free Publicity
Marcia Yudkin

Jumpstart Your Book Sales
Tom and Marilyn Ross

On the Air: How to Get on Radio and TV Talk Shows and What to Do When You Get There
Al Parinello

Persuading on Paper: The Complete Guide to Writing Copy That Pulls in Business
Marcia Yudkin

Writing

The Recipe Writer's Handbook
Barbara Gibbs Ostmann and Jane L. Baker

Your Life as Story
Tristine Rainer

Financial

Your Money or Your Life
Joe Dominguez and Vicki Robin

Index

Suggest a Publisher
For the Next Book

Do you know a small publisher who you think would be perfect for the next edition of *Make Money Self-Publishing*? What about you? Eligible publishers should meet the following two requirements:

1) Have earned a net profit of at least $20,000 for the most recent year if publishing non-fiction; $10,000 if publishing only fiction.
2) Have self-published at least one book.

In addition, publishers will be chosen based on the diversity they can add to the next edition. Publishers will be selected by how they contribute to a balance between the types of books published, the ages and genders of the publishers, the physical locations of the publishing companies, and the methods that are used to sell books.

Please realize that a suggested publisher may be acceptable in every way EXCEPT that she or he publishes cookbooks and the next book already has two cookbook publishers, or an excess of publishers have been suggested who sell primarily through gift stores, or too many nominated publishers live in California. Plus each edition of *Make Money Self-Publishing* is limited in size. So if your suggested company is not selected, that's not a negative comment. Instead it is an editorial decision made so the next edition can provide inspiration for as broad a range of readers as is possible.

However, certain types of publishers are rarer than others. Anyone who is making money self-publishing fiction, even if they are also publishing non-fiction, will be more likely to make it into the next edition. Publishers who live in places different than the publishers in this current edition will have an edge, especially someone who lives outside the United States. Publishers who are financially successful publishing illustrated books, preferably in color, are also on the wish list.

The next edition of *Make Money Self-Publishing* is scheduled to be published in the spring of 2003 with the majority of interviews taking place in the spring of 2002. Suggestions for possible publishers to interview need to be received no later than March, 2002. Please copy and complete the following form and mail it to P.O. Box 19948, Boulder, CO 80308. Or e-mail the same information with the subject line, Suggested Publisher to Interview, to PatMich170@aol.com.

Thanks for taking the time to suggest a publisher! If the suggested publisher is not you, and therefore you don't know all the answers for the questions, that's fine. Do the best you can.

If your suggested publisher is formally interviewed, even if their interview doesn't make it into the next edition, you'll receive a free copy of the next edition of *Make Money Self-Publishing*. One catch: you have to be the first person to suggest that publisher in order to get the free book. If you want to check if a publisher has already been suggested before you complete the suggestion form, send an e-mail to PatMich170@aol.com, or call Gemstone House Publishing at 303-417-9974.

Suggested Publisher to Interview

Name of publisher:_____

Address of publisher:_____

Phone number of publisher:_____

E-mail address of publisher:_____

If you are someone different than the above publisher, please also provide answers to the above four questions for yourself:_____

_____

_____

Does this person publish fiction?____What kind (for example, children's stories or romances)?_____

_____

Does this person publish non-fiction?_____What kind (for example, cookbooks or travel guides)?_____

_____

Has she or he earned over $10,000 net profit annually if publishing only fiction?_____

Has she or he earned over $20,000 net profit annually if publishing only non-fiction, or a combination of fiction and non-fiction?_____

What is the publisher's age (for example, twenties, fifties, middle-aged, senior)?_____

What is the publisher's gender?_____

What is the primary way she or he markets books?____

_____

What is the secondary way?_____

_____

Does the publisher have employees?_____
How many?_____
Does the publisher work from home or out of an office?
_____
What year was the publishing company started?_____
How many titles does the publisher have in print?_____
Has she or he published other authors?_____
How many?_____
Is there a special reason you think this publisher would interest readers? Something unique or unusual? Perhaps this publisher is younger or older than usual. Maybe he or she has done well selling books as premiums or through catalogs._____

_____
_____
_____
_____

If your suggested publisher is interviewed, and you are the first person to nominate him or her, we'll send you a free copy of the next *Make Money Self-Publishing.*To get your book, you must let us know who you are and how to contact you. We will not release your name to any outside companies.

Your name:_____
Street address:_____
City:_____ State:___ Zip Code:_____
E-mail address:_____
Phone number:_____

Order Form

To order copies of *Make Money Self-Publishing:Learn How from Fourteen Successful Small Publishers* using a credit card, call 1-800-324-6415. Or copy and mail this order form to: Gemstone House Publishing, P.O. Box 19948, Boulder, CO 80308.

Your Name: _____

Address: _____

_____

City & State: _____

Zip: _____

Phone #: _____

Discount schedule when ordering directly from publisher:

1-2 books	no discount ($19.95 ea)
3-4 books	20% ($15.96 ea)
5+ books	40% ($11.97 ea)

For large quantities, contact the publisher for discount.

Please send me _____ copies of *Make Money Self-Publishing: Learn How from Fourteen Successful Small Publishers* at

$_____ each for a total of $_____

Add $3.00 shipping for the first book $___3.00

Plus $1.00 for each additional book $_____

(Books will be shipped by United States Priority Mail)

Total: $_____

Payment is by: _____ Check or _____ Mastercard or Visa

Card #: _____   Expiration Date: ___/___

Signature: _____

What Do You Think?
Tell Us and Win a Gift!

We want each edition of this book to be as useful and helpful to small publishers as possible. To achieve that goal, we need to know what you liked, what you didn't care for, and what additional information you want us to include next time.

Completed feedback sheets will be entered in a contest to win a $20.00 bookstore gift certificate. Mail this form to P.O. Box 19948, Boulder, CO 80308. A prize will be awarded at least once per year through 2003. For updated contest information, check our web site, www.MakeMoneySelfPublishing.com.

What are your favorite three chapters? _____
Why?_____
_____

What are your least favorite three chapters?_____
Why?_____
_____

What did you think was the most valuable information in this book?_____
_____

What other information did you want to read about that wasn't included?_____
_____

To enter the contest, please complete the rest of this form.

Name:_____
Street address:_____
City:_____ State:____ Zip Code:_____
E-mail address:_____ Phone #:_____
Your favorite bookstore:_____